Galapagos

In Darwin's Footsteps

Mark Newman

ISBN:1466287713
ISBN-13:9781466287716

To Christine and Wendy

CONTENTS

ACKNOWLEDGMENTS

I would like to thank Carolyn French, without whose perceptive suggestions for revisions the twice-as-long original manuscript would still be languishing on a shelf; Terry Domico for suggesting the title for this book and for being my partner on other book projects; Tony Dawson, for getting me up to speed with computers and for being, as he calls it, my "disc doctor"; my artistic sister, Wendy, for her invaluable help with the map graphics and for the scanning of historical photos; Juan Vera for showing me the wildlife and explaining the natural features of the various islands that we visited; the Charles Darwin Foundation and the Galapagos National Park Service for their extraordinary efforts to preserve the Galapagos ecosystem, most recently demonstrated by the success of Project Isabela; Dave McCargo for being a good traveling companion and a good sport; and my then-wife, Kathy, for putting up with my travels as best as she could. And special thanks to Mark Eisenstadt for a final proofreading and editing of the manuscript and for his various suggestions on how to improve it. This is the second time he's come to my rescue. Also thanks again to Maureen Cutajar in Malta for formatting the manuscript.

FOREWORD

Like Darwin's finches, this book has gone through its own evolution. It began as a field journal written during my January-to-March trip to the Galapagos in 1996.

Writing in the Kofa Mountains and at Lake Havasu in Arizona, and then in Haines and Anchorage in Alaska, I worked the journal notes into a 275 page travel narrative with no illustrations.

After that came innumerable rewrites following the suggestions first of my original agent, Ivy Stone, and more recently Carolyn French. Carolyn told me that writing is all about *rewriting*. The manuscript shrank significantly in length and came to include a number of my photographs. Final revisions were undertaken in Whitehorse in the Yukon, and in Woodside and San Francisco in California.

In order to survive, the Galapagos tortoise adapted to unique environmental challenges, forming fourteen different races. My book, in undergoing multiple changes over a 15 year period, has adapted to the realities of the publishing landscape.

I hope you enjoy the book in its current state of evolution.

Whitehorse, Yukon Territory

September 2011

Mark Newman

"Traveling makes men wiser, but they learn new habits which cannot be gratified when they return home."

Thomas Jefferson 1789, Paris

"It is not the strongest of the species that survive, nor the most intelligent, but the one most responsive to change."

Charles Darwin

"Not all who wander are lost"

JRR Tolkien

Culpepper

Wenman

The Galápagos Islands

Pinta

Marchena

Genovesa

Equator

Santiago

Bartolomé

Seymour Norte

B

R

Fernandina

Santa Cruz

San Cristóbal

P

Isabela

Santa Fe

T

0 MILES 50

Floreana

Española

B Baltra P Pinzón R Rábida T Tortuga

Chapter One
DARWIN & THE GALAPAGOS CALL

I have been a professional wildlife photographer for over thirty years. I had already spent time photographing on all seven continents when I decided to visit the Galapagos Islands. With my having a passion for adventure and travel in addition to an enthusiasm for capturing new and exotic photographic imagery, it's a wonder that I hadn't traveled there sooner. In addition to my wildlife quest, I was also fascinated by Charles Darwin's scientific voyage to the islands aboard the *H.M.S. Beagle* in 1835. Although it is a different place today than in the 19th century, much of the Galapagos ecosystem remains intact. I hoped it would still be possible to experience some of what

Darwin encountered on his long-ago journey, and in that sense to walk in his footsteps.

I invited a friend, Dave McCargo, to accompany me on the adventure. In the past we had traveled together to places such as Borneo and Australia's outback, and I knew he was dependable and good at working out logistics.

Darwin never had the luxury of choosing his traveling companions. He was invited on the *Beagle's* five-year voyage by the ship's captain, and it was a matter of either take it or leave it. Darwin suffered much during the long voyage, both emotionally and physically. If he had had a buddy along he might have fared a good deal better.

The Galapagos Islands, lying 576 miles off the coast of Ecuador, occupy a land mass half as large as Hawaii. The islands drift slowly from northwest to southeast over an ocean floor volcanic hotspot that spews molten lava, sporadically resulting in full-blown eruptions on the surface of the two most westerly islands of the archipelago, Isabela and Fernandina.

Isabela was the third island of the archipelago that Darwin visited. The fact that he had time only to survey the island but not to climb to the tops of any of its five tall volcanoes made me eager to explore even beyond the realm of what Darwin had seen. I knew that *Sierra Negra*, the third highest volcano on Isabela, was climbable and readily accessible. Darwin had noticed steam coming from the top of one of the volcanoes — probably *Sierra Negra*-- and mentioned that observation in his diary entry for September 29, 1835.

The Galapagos Islands formed *de novo*, that is to say, they had never been attached to a mainland continent. Because their distance from South America is so substantial, the flora and fauna that came to inhabit these ocean up thrusts were able, over many tens of thousands of years, to develop into races that are unique in all the world.

Charles Darwin was the first person to bring the phenomenon of the diversity of these races to world attention in any meaningful way. He wasn't, however, the first one to notice the diversity. That distinction belongs to Nicolas Lawson, the Governor of Floreana Island during Darwin's visit. But Darwin was the first to capitalize on that knowledge. During his five-year voyage aboard the ninety-foot ship, the *Beagle*, he only spent an astonishingly short five weeks in the Galapagos, visiting only four of the islands. The year was 1835.

Those five weeks proved to be perhaps the most momentous field time ever engaged in by a naturalist. Based in large part on his resulting observations, twenty-four years later, in 1859, Darwin published his revolutionary bombshell, *On The Origin of Species.*

If it wasn't for Darwin, the Galapagos Islands today would arguably be just another jumble of obscure, black rocks jutting above the ocean's surface. Instead, the islands have been elevated to National Park status (1959) by the government of Ecuador and to World Heritage Site status (1979) by the United Nations

(UNESCO). In addition, they are the focus of ongoing scientific scrutiny by the international conservation community and a model demonstration of the benefits of ecotourism. The Galapagos provides for the sustainable influx of over two hundred million tourist dollars into the Ecuadorian economy every year.

If it hadn't been for Charles Darwin, I probably would have visited Baja or perhaps Costa Rica instead of the Galapagos. Without Darwin's legacy it is highly unlikely that my travel agent could have so routinely come up with plane tickets for this so isolated of Pacific locations. Over thirty jets land in the Galapagos each week.

Our plane landed at the ex-military airport of Baltra on January 31 in the central Galapagos Islands. Baltra is a small, flat island, just over ten square miles in area, that was used by the United States military during World War II for strategic purposes. The ruins of old concrete bunkers now rest silently beneath the hot equatorial sun. After the war, the island was returned to the Ecuadorian government. Today the U.S.-built airport is the main access point for tourists arriving from Quito and Guayaquil on the Ecuadorian mainland.

A two hour bus-ferry-bus shuttle takes visitors from the Baltra Airport to the main harbor and population center of the Galapagos Islands, Puerto Ayora. This cozy little town lies at the southern end of Santa Cruz Island which, at 380 square miles, is the second largest island in the archipelago after Isabela. Darwin, however, never made landfall on either Santa Cruz or Baltra.

The first thing on my mind upon arriving in Baltra was to locate a boat that could take us around the archipelago and put us in contact with the extraordinary wildlife.

When Charles Darwin arrived in the Galapagos in September of 1835 he had no such logistical problem. He already had a boat, the *H.M.S. Beagle*. And he wasn't particularly looking for animals. What first captured his attention and engaged his enormous imagination were geological features, not the flora and fauna. His initial descriptions were of volcanic rocks, craters, and climate — not of animals and birds. Robert Fitzroy, captain of the *Beagle*, had wanted a geologist for the expedition. So he asked his friends at Cambridge University to recommend someone and they suggested Darwin.

Geology was not a formal degreed discipline at the time. Fitzroy, in order to help supplement Darwin's knowledge, gave him a copy of Charles Lyell's *Principles of Geology* for the voyage. Darwin was neither a biologist nor a geologist. Instead, he had studied theology after being pressured into that field by his father.

On September 17, 1835, when the *Beagle* anchored off Chatham Island (today known as San Cristobal), Darwin's description of what he saw was less than enthusiastic. He wrote, "Nothing could be less inviting than the first appearance. We fancied even that the bushes smelt unpleasantly."

By the time Dave McCargo and I reached the Galapagos in 1996, it was 161 years after Darwin's visit. The world's perspective on these amazing islands had changed dramatically. The rocks and hillsides, except for a few farms and roads here and there, were pretty much the same as in 1835. But instead of being viewed as a wasteland of uninviting desolation, the Galapagos today is thought of as an amazing outdoor laboratory, teeming with unique and bizarre forms of wildlife found nowhere else.

In 1959 the government of Ecuador designated 97%

of the land area of the Galapagos Islands as national park. Only 1% of that area is open to tourists, the rest being totally protected.

While a boat is necessary to be able to experience all of the different life forms of the remote outlying islands, one's wildlife encounters begin almost from the moment of touchdown at the Baltra airport.

Amidst the commotion of suitcases, backpacks, and jet-lagged tourists scurrying for buses at the northeast corner of Santa Cruz Island, the observant traveler can immediately catch glimpses of a whole array of sea birds.

The first exotic-looking species I spotted was the storm petrel, a small black bird with a white rump patch. A flock of these birds plied the narrow channel between Baltra and Santa Cruz, looking for tiny fish scraps amongst the anchored boats.

I spied two kinds of herons, reminiscent of Florida waterways, standing motionless amongst the red mangrove roots not one hundred feet from where the first bus began to load passengers. One was a great blue heron, an enormous gray bird, standing four feet tall, with a long, snake-like neck, a beak pointed like a spear, and a wingspan of six feet. The other bird, a yellow-crowned night heron, had a comical look about it, with a black and white horizontally-banded head. It had big eyes which helped its night vision, but which gave the bird a startled look during the day.

In Puerto Ayora Dave and I booked passage on an old brigantine schooner named the *Angelique* that would take us around to some of the islands. Then I strolled down the street, not surprisingly named *Avenida Charles Darwin*, to a fish-cleaning station. Fishermen were busy attending to their day's catch, occasionally tossing out scraps which attracted a cloud of frigatebirds and a few blue-footed boobies.

The Galapagos Islands are home to two of the world's five species of frigatebirds — the great frigatebird, *Fregata minor,* and the magnificent frigatebird, *Fregata magnificens.* Even serious birders say they are not easy to distinguish from each other. With slender, seven-foot black wings and precision flying, the birds were impressive to me no matter what their genus and species. They were incredible acrobats as they swooped down to grab fish scraps.

On some large rocks to the left of the fish-cleaning

canopy, two adult marine iguanas basked in the hot sun. I slowly and quietly approached and was able to sit down within three feet of the pair without disturbing them at all. These sea-going iguanas, which evolved from the land forms, are the most primeval-looking of the vast array of Galapagos creatures. They conjure up the notion of dinosaurs and evoke thoughts of the far distant past. They are a photographer's delight and the closer you get, the more impressive they look.

Darwin must have been in a bad mood when he wrote of them, "It is a hideous-looking creature, stupid, and sluggish in movements."

As I sat and observed the iguanas, I saw them as the embodiment of ancient-ness, the defining ingredient of a prehistoric world. A single frame-filling photograph of the head and spine-covered neck of a marine iguana says more about past ages than a dozen books on the subject.

I had a daypack with me in which I carried my camera and a 35-200mm zoom lens, giving me an optical multiplication factor of up to four times. I took out the camera and gradually maneuvered the lens to within one foot of the face of one of the iguanas. He tolerated me, but did seem to go into a high-alert mode, doing a push-up with his head raised, and pointing his head straight at me.

Marine Iguana

Then he sneezed and I could feel the spray on my face.

I subsequently learned that sneezing is the mechanism used by these iguanas to excrete salt. Their diet of seaweed gives them a high salt intake. To cope, they have the most efficient salt gland of any reptile in the world. The glands are located above their eyes, and are connected to their nostrils by a duct. When an iguana sneezes it shoots salt out of its nostril. Usually this puff of salt lands on its own head, giving it a whitish appearance as puff after puff accumulates. Sometimes, though, the salty sneeze lands squarely in the face of an overenthusiastic photographer.

It is always a special honor when any form of wildlife allows one to approach closely and does not flee. The exotic location of these islands leant a fairytale aspect to my initial meeting with the iguanas. Many more such encounters were soon to follow. I felt like I was entering a dream world — a *Peaceable Kingdom* — where animals didn't run away, sea creatures didn't swim away, and birds didn't fly away.

Even though it was still early in the 19th century when he visited here, Darwin did have a camera along on his voyage. It was a pioneering Graflex model. But he chose not to use it very often, and he and his crewmates instead pursued other less benign endeavors. One of the more perverted games that they came up with was called 'dunking the iguana'. Darwin did not actively participate, although neither did he interfere. He was a passive accomplice.

Always an observant scientist, he watched without protest as a fellow seaman tied an iguana to a weighted line and lowered the unfortunate creature below the surface. It was a grisly experiment in drowning. Under normal circumstances when feeding on seaweed, iguanas usually stay submerged for no longer than ten minutes. The line was kept down for a full hour before being raised. To Darwin's and everyone's amazement, when it was finally brought up, the marine iguana was not only alive, but still very active.

Perhaps this kind of activity was to be expected from a boatload of men who required a flogging for drunken behavior. The very next day after setting sail from England, when the *Beagle* was barely underway, Captain Fitzroy ordered 134 lashes doled out to about a quarter of the crew.

Darwin wrote in his journal that he threw one of the iguanas as far as he could into a deep tidal pool. He mentions that the animal swam back to shore and tried to shuffle away but, "I several times caught the same lizard, and as often as I threw it in, it returned to shore."

One can only wonder whether, if Darwin had paid more attention to photography, perhaps he could have developed more of an artistic sense and dispensed with the need to amuse himself by tossing and attempting to drown iguanas.

Charles Darwin in 1838 (watercolor by G. Richmond)

I decided I had been sneezed upon one too many times and backed off from the iguana that I had been photographing.

The bird activity around the nearby fishermen was still frantic. Three pelicans had joined the commotion of the feeding frenzy. Two stood on the gunwale of an old wooden skiff anchored near shore. The third pelican perched in a red mangrove bush. One of the pelicans on the boat looked like he was choking and repeatedly threw his head back as if trying to clear his throat. He had apparently swallowed an oversized meal which lent a grotesque appearance to his neck. Over the next weeks I often observed this same phenomenon of near-choking and finally accepted that a pelican's eyes are bigger than its esophagus. Somehow these mega-meals always seemed to pass successfully sooner or later, with the pelicans left none the worse for wear.

The choking episodes were more traumatic for the human observer than for the hungry bird.

There are eight species of pelicans in the world with only one, the brown pelican, living in the Galapagos. This same species, which also lives in North America, was once classified as endangered in parts of the United States.

Chapter Two
THE ANGELIQUE

The ship we had booked passage on, the *Angelique*, was a ninety-six foot brigantine schooner. At 9 PM on a Friday night, Dave and I carried our gear down to Puerto Ayora's main dock. The place was bustling, with open skiffs shuttling groups of travelers to and fro between the various anchored tour boats and shore. In Darwin's time whalers and pirates plied these waters. Now there were tour boats.

In the crowd of about seventy or eighty people on the dock, the twelve of us about to embark on the voyage of the *Angelique* eventually found each other. It required two half-hour shuttles in a twenty-foot tender, known as a *panga* in Spanish, to get all the gear and people aboard the big schooner which was anchored some distance from the main dock.

I went with the second relay and sat in the bow of the tender, next to a short, slightly-built Ecuadorian of about thirty-five. His name was Juan Vera. Juan told us that he was going to be our trip naturalist and leader. As we motored along, a few birds flew over us. In the dark I couldn't make out what they were as they passed by like speeding shadows.

We pulled alongside the *Angelique* and everyone climbed up the ship's ladder. Then the skiff was hoisted onto the back deck with pulleys and the ladder was hauled up.

The six crew members had their own quarters, and we twelve passengers, all paired up in one fashion or another, had six rooms amongst us. This was true luxury compared with Charles Darwin's accommodations.

The three-masted *Beagle* was six feet shorter than the *Angelique*, had only two cabins, and yet carried seventy-six crew members. The five year voyage was so crowded and cramped that Darwin felt compelled to remark, "The absolute want of room is an evil that nothing can surmount."

H.M.S. *Beagle* in Straits of Magellan. Mt. Sarmiento in the distance.

(Drawing done in 1889-1890, Artist Unknown, depicts ship well before reaching the Galapagos)

Darwin, being six feet tall, had to stoop when inside his shared living quarters. When he went to bed, he had to remove a drawer from a locker to make room for his feet. Add to that his frequent bouts with seasickness and claustrophobia and it's no wonder he came to write, "I loathe, I abhor the sea, and all ships which sail on it."

While the *Angelique's* crew made ready for departure, we all hauled our gear below deck. Dave and I shared a cabin and I claimed the upper bunk. It had its own fan and light. The cabin was about six feet wide by ten feet long. That included a closet, double-decker bunk, and a bathroom.

Darwin's cabin, by comparison, was ten by eleven, and he had to share that space with two other crew members-- 19 year old John Stokes, and 14 year old Philip King. Can you imagine sharing such a diminutive living space with two teenagers for an extended voyage? For a seven-day cruise one can tolerate a cramped situation. But for *five years*? It's unimaginable. It is fairly amazing that Darwin endured for the entire trip. He had many psychological and physical obstacles, yet he fought back his demons and persisted.

One thing that Darwin did have in common with adventure travelers from his or any other age were skeptical parents. He was verbally pummeled by his father both before and during the voyage (there was mail service at certain ports of call). His father didn't want him to participate, calling the trip a "wild scheme" and a "useless undertaking," after which he'd "never settle down to a steady life." Those are the same sentiments that many of us travelers have heard from our own parents for years.

Of course Darwin's father could not have been more incorrect. As a successful doctor in Victorian

England, Robert Darwin feared his son was on the hipster path to nowhere. "You care for nothing," he admonished Charles, "but shooting, dogs, and rat-catching, and you will be a disgrace to yourself and all your family."

It's always pleasing to me when a victimized adventurous spirit comes to have the last laugh.

At midnight, our captain, Franklin Angemeyer, started up the engine and the *Angelique* motored due South.

When I awoke at dawn, we were just pulling up to anchor at the northern tip of Floreana Island. At 67 square miles, Floreana, known as "Charles" in Darwin's time, is the sixth largest of the Galapagos Islands. It was the second of four islands that Darwin visited. He made landfall there on September 23, 1835, his eighth day in the Galapagos. San Cristobal was the first island visited by the *Beagle*. However, since it was sixty miles to the northeast of Floreana, it was too far off track to be included on our current itinerary.

The *Beagle* had made a clockwise sweep through the islands, from San Cristobal to Floreana to Isabela and finally to Santiago.

What Darwin encountered on Floreana was an Ecuadorian penal colony comprised of 250 prisoners, a Vice-governor by the name of Nicholas Lawson, and plenty of tortoises which were a mainstay of the prisoners' diets.

When our party went ashore at Punta Cormorant on Floreana we saw a green sand beach, about sixty tourists, and no tortoises.

A quarter mile walk with Juan Vera leading the way brought our group to a white sand beach with many green sea turtles swimming within meters of shore. A few of us waded thigh deep into the clear, calm water, and then stood perfectly still. Several white-tipped reef sharks swam by within inches of our legs. Juan assured us that this species of shark never attacks humans.

One of the sea turtles remained on shore, at the water's edge, facing out toward the ocean. She had laid her eggs a few hundred feet inland, above the high tide line, sometime during the night. You have to wonder how a small-brained turtle can figure out high tide lines when most of us can barely make sense out of a published tide table chart. Be that as it may, the sea turtle, having demonstrated her intuitive genius for gauging water levels, now readied herself for a return to the sea. The beach had many of the distinctive wide deep tracks left by turtles that had already reentered the ocean.

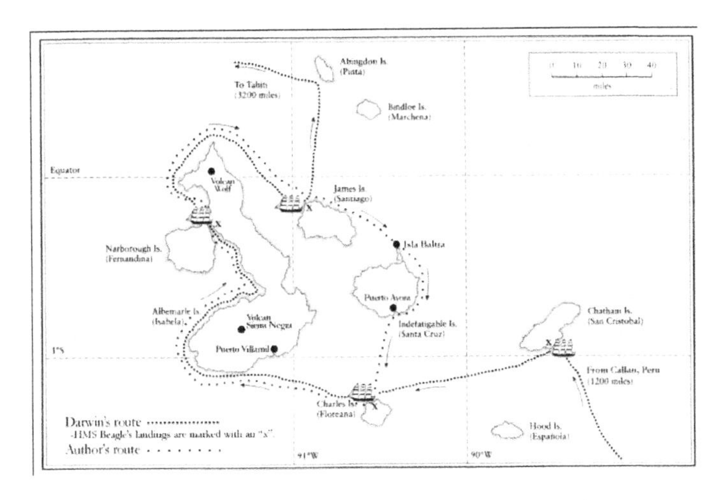

I walked down the beach, away from my shipmates, and sat down near a group of bright, colorful, red and blue Sally lightfoot crabs. These crabs are remarkably tamer on Floreana than on the populated island of Santa Cruz. I sat still and a dozen crabs approached very closely. It is said that this species is capable of running across the surface of the water, although I personally never observed such a phenomenon.

Juan Vera was one of a limited number of Park Service naturalist guides. By Ecuadorian law, every tour boat must have a guide aboard, and passengers are never allowed ashore without that guide as an escort.

Sally Lightfoot Crab

Juan was bright, enthusiastic, and conscientious. He treated his work like a calling, not just a job. When he found a bleached-out turtle skull lying on the beach, he held it up to the group, giving us a spontaneous chelonian anatomy lesson.

I found over the course of the next days that he was never content to give just a minimal explanation about anything; he would always punctuate his dissertations with either a personal anecdote or else a joke. As a case in point, he finished the turtle skull seminar with the following words of wisdom, referring to how we should act if we were to come across turtle eggs on the beach:

"Please don't shake it,
Please don't break it,
It took mama and papa
A long time to make it."

We walked back to the green sand beach where we had come ashore. On the way we passed by a lagoon off to the left side of the trail. Through eight-power binoculars I could see a single pair of the archipelago's five hundred greater flamingos. They were standing on the far side of the lagoon. The lagoon contains small shrimp and crabs, as well as an aquatic insect called the "water boatman," all of which make up the flamingo's diet. I could not find any reference in Darwin's diary indicating that he had seen flamingos. Maybe they are a relatively new arrival to the archipelago, like the cattle egret.

Closer to our side of the lagoon, a pair of black-necked stilts, a black and white wading bird with spindly red legs, could be seen poking their backs below the water's surface and into the mud, probing for food. A few graceful white-cheeked pintail ducks, and a group of migratory whimbrels with long curved bills could be seen scattered across the shallows.

Juan Vera giving a natural history talk to shipmates on Floreana Island

We returned to the *Angelique*, had lunch and then took the panga out to a semicircle of rocks not far offshore from Floreana, called "Devil's Crown."

Floreana has some of the best dive sites in the Galapagos and Devil's Crown is one of them. Most tour boats take time to let their passengers snorkel here. The water is surprisingly cool for being on the equator. This is due to the Humboldt Current. Before we jumped into the water, the panga circled around the rocks and we were able to observe herons, lava gulls, and brown pelicans.

Hammerhead sharks live in these waters. In other

seas of the world the hammerhead is considered dangerous, yet in the Galapagos this creature, like many of the other forms of wildlife here, has a tolerance for humans. There have been no recorded shark attacks in the Galapagos. Sharks here are simply not aggressive towards people.

Swimming was probably the last thing on Darwin's mind when he visited Floreana. In his diary entry for September 24, 1835, he wrote that the inland settlement then existing on the island was only "five to six years standing." He mentions seeing plantains and potatoes growing and wrote, "The inhabitants here lead sort of a Robinson Crusoe life; the houses are very simple, built of poles and thatched with grass. Part of their time is employed in hunting the wild pigs and goats with which the woods abound."

On September 25, after Governor Lawson visited a whaling vessel, Darwin recorded that "...on an average in the year 60-70 Whaling vessels call for provisions & refreshment." Mainly, the vessels collected tortoises which they kept alive on board. Lawson told Darwin that he could determine which island a tortoise had come from by the shape of its shell. At the time,

Darwin did not pay much attention to what Lawson was telling him. However, in later years that information would have profound ramifications. Darwin was so unmoved with regard to any information about the giant tortoises that he failed to collect even a single adult specimen to bring back to England. The only tortoises the crew collected were for meat (plus three live babies to bring home).

After an hour of snorkeling, we shuttled back to the ship, raised the anchor, set the sails, and headed northwest toward the island of Isabela. A few frigatebirds joined our cruise, sitting high up on the yardarm of the masts.

Once underway, our group of twelve pulled up lounge chairs on the forward deck and looked toward the reddening western sky as the sun dipped lower toward the horizon. The day gave up some of its warmth as dusk approached and the *Angelique* danced its way toward Elizabeth Bay, 114 miles distant, on the concave western side of Isabela Island.

At 3 PM the following afternoon we pulled into the bay and dropped anchor.

The *Beagle* also headed to Isabela (Albemarle) Island

from Floreana . On September 28, 1835, Darwin wrote in his diary, "Steered toward the southern end of Albemarle Isd., which was surveyed." The main task of the *Beagle* was actually surveying and not zoological research.

Isabela Island, shaped something like a prehistoric stone fishhook, is the largest island in the archipelago, occupying nearly sixty percent of the Galapagos land mass. Both it and neighboring Fernandina Island to its west are visited much less often than the other islands in the chain.

Darwin made landfall on September 29, 1835 and anchored at noon. He was about two weeks into his Galapagos travels and it was the third island that he had visited. The *Beagle* had stopped in a location now called Tagus Cove, a preferred anchorage site for pirates and whalers. From there the crew took a dinghy ashore. Darwin wrote that the cove was beneath "the highest & boldest land which we have yet seen."

Once on Albemarle, Darwin and the crew quickly proceeded to kill iguanas. He writes in his journal, "The rocks on the coast abounded with great black lizards, between three and four feet long; and on the hills, an ugly yellowish-brown species was equally common." The latter species he is referring to is the land iguana. Darwin goes on to call them "singularly stupid in appearance."

Land Iguana

When our entourage stepped ashore at the exact same location, we didn't see a single iguana of the marine or land variety. Yet despite Darwin's stating that, "The whole of this part of Albemarle Island is miserably sterile, "we managed to enjoy ourselves, wandering around the stark landscape just inland from the cove. An easy trail led above a large, circular, brackish lake that Darwin had hiked down to sixteen decades earlier. He had hoped to find fresh water in the lake. Having read his journals I already knew that the water was not drinkable.

The lake may have had water too salty to drink, but the site was certainly picturesque. If Darwin had had more of an artistic leaning and had paid some more attention to using his Graflex camera, his outlook on the scene before him would have been more positive. In addition, there would have been a photographic record left to posterity. But apparently he had little aesthetic sense and to him all was about science, killing, and collecting.

The trail continued upward to a vantage from which we had an expansive view across a large lava field. We could see the 4350 ft. volcano to the north that now bore Darwin's name. On October 1st, Darwin wrote that Albemarle "is composed of 6 or 7 great Volcanic Mounds from 2 to 3000 ft. high." Although Darwin had the number of volcanoes correct (there are six), he had underestimated their altitudes. Wolf Volcano tops out at 5600 feet.

To me, the most interesting aspect of the lowland terrain were the hillsides covered with palo santo trees. These light colored, skeletal-appearing trees are very drought resistant. They space themselves out relatively uniformly across the gentle slopes, reminding one of a French impressionistic painting. It is likely that Darwin looked out upon a nearly identical scene but if he had any appreciation of the rugged landscape, he gave no indication of it in his writings.

We remained anchored in Tagus Cove for the night, noting the graffiti on the cliffs around the shore from the crews of ships long gone.

Early the following morning, the *Angelique* crossed the six miles to Punta Espinosa on the northeastern tip of Fernandina Island. Fernandina is the youngest of the Galapagos Islands and consists of a single large volcano that is still active, called Volcan La Cumbre, which is 4800 feet high. Some scientists think that Fernandina is not much more than 100,000 years old (Isabela is one million). In geologic time, that is almost nothing. Both Isabela and Fernandina are still in the active process of rising.

Punta Espinosa has the greatest concentration of marine iguanas in all the islands. The sight of them is overwhelming.

Photographer and Marine Iguanas at Punta Espinosa

Many thousands group together en mass seeking to stay warm. They lay on the beach all facing in the same direction, towards the sun. There are so many iguanas that when you walk around you have to be careful not to step on them. Although marine iguanas are found throughout the archipelago, they grow to their largest size on the islands of Isabela and Fernandina. Adult males can grow to over 4 ft. in length and weigh up to 3.3 pounds.

I was so excited by the concentration of iguanas that it was difficult to understand Darwin's attitude in 1835. He was not at all enamored of this unique seagoing lizard. Back then he wrote, "The black lava rocks are frequented by large, most disgusting clumsy Lizards.

They are black as the rocks over which they crawl." The more I thought about Darwin, the more I wondered how such an intellectual talent could be so unable to appreciate the beauty of nature.

The iguana gathering is the most obvious attention grabber at *Punta Espinosa*, but the real stars of Fernandina are the flightless cormorants. This unique, endemic species is found only around the westernmost islands and nowhere else in the Galapagos, let alone any other place in the world.

I tagged along at the rear of our group so I could take some time for photographing. Juan was at the head of the procession handing out morsels of information along the way. We crossed over some sandy areas where marine iguanas were nesting in the holes that they had excavated. One iguana, almost entirely covered with sand, popped its head out of a burrow. I snapped a shot fast, before it had a chance to duck back in. There were so many nesting burrows that it was difficult to avoid trampling over them. The iguanas above ground usually scampered out of the way, but several times my foot was about to come down on one when at the last instant I would notice its presence and halt my stride.

At the end of the trail on a low rock along the waterfront, a flightless cormorant stood resting. Of the twenty-eight species of cormorants in the world this is the only one found in the Galapagos and the only cormorant that is unable to fly. It has developed strong legs for swimming instead of strong wings for flying and has evolved into a swimming bird in much the same way as the penguin, which also lives here.

The flightless cormorant is a medium-sized black and brown bird, with blue eyes and tiny, non-functional stubby wing remnants. This cormorant not only has stunted wings, but it has even lost the part of its breastbone to which wing muscles normally attach. It feeds within 330 ft. of shore on fish, squid, octopus and eels. There are only about eight hundred pairs of flightless cormorants in existence, with all of them living around Isabela and Fernandina islands.

Even though it is unable to fly, the flightless cormorant apparently still thinks it is a normal bird, because it tries to dry its "wings," if you could call them

Flightless Cormorants
(Painting by JG Keulemans)

that, in the same fashion as its better-endowed relatives. These cormorants appear comical as they hold their vestigial wing stubs spread out away from their sides in order to allow the sun and breeze to dry them.

A few unconcerned sea lions napped within meters of the cormorant. The bird was entirely trusting and I was able to put the camera's lens within eighteen inches of the cormorant's face without causing any disturbance.

When Juan figured we had spent enough time taking

photographs, he herded the group back through the iguana masses to the boat launch area, from which we shuttled by panga back to the ship.

The next leg of our journey was to take us one hundred miles, first north across the equator, then east across the top of Isabela Island, and finally south to Santiago Island.

Sailing north in the *Beagle* on October 30, 1835, Darwin noted steam coming from one of the craters on Isabela Island. After the *Angelique* tour I would return to Isabela to explore the top of one the five volcanoes on the island and see a number of steam vents up close.

We had the luxury of carrying aboard our ship all the food and water we required. For the crew of the *Beagle* obtaining fresh drinking water was sometimes a problem. On October 1, 1835, water had to be rationed, "..1/2 a Gallon for cooking & all purposes," according to Darwin. They had hoped to find water in Tagus Cove, but found only the brine pond that we had visited. On that same day, Darwin wrote in his journal about finding "a great Lizard" (the land iguana) in great numbers. He describes it as inhabiting burrows and being "quick & clumsy." He goes on to write, "They are colored an orange yellow, with the hinder part of their back brick red." Over three dozen were killed that day.

The *Angelique* rounded the north end of Santiago Island sometime in the middle of the night, and before sunrise we dropped anchor off the northwest coast of tiny Bartolome Island.

Land Iguana

In October 1835, due to wind and strong currents, the *Beagle* made a slow passage southeastward to Santiago. After a few days of no diary entries at all, on October 8th Darwin wrote that they reached James Island and that he and five others were put ashore with provisions and instructed to wait until the ship returned from a trip to Chatham Island to obtain drinking water. Chatham had been the *Beagle's* first landfall in the Galapagos on September 15.

Juan Vera had us all up at the crack of dawn, rushed us through breakfast, and got us into the panga and over to Bartolome's shore where we started hiking up a path called the Summit Trail.

The trail ascends to 374 ft. above the beach utilizing a series of long, wooden boardwalks and stairs with hand railings. The end of the trail is the highest point on the island. We were the first tourists up the trail that day and the only ones to see the most famous vista in all the Galapagos -- Pinnacle Rock surrounded by Sullivan Bay-- in warm, early-morning light. When our group had its fill of summit views and photographs, we descended to another trail leading across the western isthmus of Bartolome to a turtle nesting beach on the south side of the diminutive island.

A female Pacific green sea turtle was making her way slowly through the sand toward the water's edge as we arrived. Female green sea turtles come ashore only to lay eggs. The males live their entire lives at sea and never need make landfall.

I would have liked to photograph the turtle, but the commotion of the twelve of us hurried the large reptile into the ocean.

View from the top of Summit Trail on Bartolome Island, overlooking Sullivan Bay

The *Angelique* was conveniently anchored between two islands -- Bartolome to the east, and Santiago to the west. From the ship's deck could be seen a white islet to the north, perhaps one mile away. Many birds used that volcanic outcropping as a resting area. It is unusual to see white rock in a region covered by black lava. The name of the islet in Spanish is *Caca Roca*; it was an almost solid mass of bird guano.

Vincente, the panga driver, motored us toward shore. We passed near a pair of mating sea turtles. They looked like floating logs. In the world of sea turtles, the smaller male always takes the top position and depends on the larger, swimming female to make all the necessary movements to achieve the coupling. We left the pair alone and continued to shore, scrambling out on to the black lava rocks of Santiago Island.

Santiago is the fourth largest of the Galapagos Islands, and the fourth and final island that Darwin explored from land. After Santiago, Darwin's explorations continued in Tahiti. In all, Darwin spent five weeks in the Galapagos, with three of those weeks being on land, including nine days on Santiago. The *Beagle* made landfall there on October 8, twelve days before Darwin's final departure from the archipelago.

Darwin was put ashore with a crewmate named Bynoe, some servants, supplies, and a tent. Captain Fitzroy and the *Beagle* left them there and sailed back to San Cristobal Island where they knew there was fresh water to resupply the ship.

There were a few people working on Santiago Island in 1835, sent by Governor Lawson from Floreana Island to catch tortoises and salt the meat. Today, the entire island is protected parkland and off limits to human habitation. Darwin encountered some of those isolated people during his camping outing. Looking today at photographs of Darwin as an old sage in his

70's, with his long white beard and black hat, it is hard to really imagine him as a young man raising hell. But on Santiago, when he was only twenty-six years old, he was quite uninhibited in his activities. He lived entirely upon tortoise meat and rode around on the backs of tortoises. He even managed to find the skull of a murdered sea captain, the victim of the crew of a sealing vessel that had visited the island a few years before Darwin's arrival.

Darwin wrote that the islands were useless for any large animals. He would have been surprised to know that a century later, sixty thousand feral goats and thousands of pigs and donkeys had made Santiago their home.

Juan led the group of us across large lava fields. The lava was of the "pahoehoe" variety, named after the Hawaiian word for rope, and was formed by the surface layer cooling and slowing faster than the lava beneath it. The lava flowing underneath caused the solidifying surface to buckle thereby forming the interesting "ropy" shapes. The uneroded expanse of lava that we traversed was less than one hundred years old. Although the eastern Galapagos Islands are four million years old, fresh lava can make its way to the surface at any time. Darwin's visit had taken place seventy years before the lava field in front of us had come into existence.

Crossing the lava fields on Santiago Island

Plants referred to as "pioneers" could be seen coming right up out of the old hardened lava. It's anybody's guess what this landscape will look like in another hundred or two hundred years. In this geologically dynamic part of the world you can't even depend on rocks to remain the same. There could be new lava or the region could be vegetated over. The land here is ever-changing.

Galapagos Sea Lions on Santiago Island (The Angelique is in the background)

When we came to a small sandy beach, we found a pair of young sea lions lounging in a shallow tidal pool. Two women from our group lay in the pool right next to the sea lions who seemed to like the attention.

Galapagos Sea Lion and Sally Lightfoot Crab

Off to the side of the pool was a low rock ledge and on it another sea lion lay asleep on its back. I approached quietly to within two feet. He opened one eye briefly and then went right back to sleep. Just then a Sally lightfoot crab, also known as the red lava crab, came out of a crack in the rock and walked along the ledge and right up to the sea lion's bristly whiskers. The sea lion opened its eye again, took another quick peek, and closed it. I very slowly lifted my camera with a wide-angle lens attached. Looking through the viewfinder, I clicked off several shots before the crab panicked at the motion and ran back to its hiding place.

We were soon underway toward our next destination, comfortably fed and with all the fresh water we cared to drink. Darwin's visit to Santiago was more precarious. He wrote that while collecting "all sorts of Specimens" and camping and awaiting the return of the *Beagle*, their only source of fresh water was a little well very close to the beach. Some time between October 12th and 16th "a long Swell from the Northward having set in, the surf broke over and spoiled the fresh water." Luckily for their party of six, an American Whaler showed up and gave them three casks of water (plus a bucket of onions). The water was particularly welcome in light of the fact that the temperature in their tents was 93F (34C). Ground temperature was much hotter. A thermometer placed in the sand "immediately rose to 137F (58C); & how much higher it would have done I do not know: for it was not graduated above this."

As we motored along in the late afternoon toward North Seymour Island, I thought of Darwin's health problems, which began even before the voyage of the *Beagle* and lasted for over forty years. Darwin complained that, "I never pass 24 hours without many hours of discomfort." As a wildlife photographer with hiking and traveling an integral part of my career, good health is a prerequisite and I feel very fortunate in having never had any serious ailments.

Darwin's situation was quite different. He had lots of disease symptoms, and they had a profound effect on his ability to work and function socially. At home in England after the voyage he was only able to work from 8-9:30 A.M., and again from 10:30 to noon. That's only a three-hour work day. He had skin rashes, heart palpitations, abdominal pain, dizziness, and headaches on a regular basis.

Darwin was troubled by some of these problems during the time of his voyage, and all of them from about age thirty until his death in 1882 at the age of 73. He consulted with more than twenty doctors but the cause of his medical condition was never definitively diagnosed.

What scholars now think is that Darwin may have contracted *Chaga's* disease, also known as trypanosomiasis, somewhere in South America. He spent a good deal of time ashore on the South American coast during the *Beagle's* long voyage, and had ample opportunity to become infected by the protozoan parasite, *Trypanosoma cruzi*. The disease is transmitted to humans by various species of bugs. The parasite affects mainly the heart and intestines, and can explain most, if not all, of Darwin's symptoms. Once infected, you are stuck with the disease for life. To this day, there is no good treatment, especially in the chronic phase of the illness.

Whatever the cause of Darwin's compromised health, his enormous productivity could have been greater yet had his constitution been more robust.

The night sky was clear as we motored along.

We dropped anchor off the south shore of North Seymour Island some time before midnight.

The entire Galapagos archipelago consists of thirteen large islands, six small ones, and about forty tiny "islets." Most tour companies visit a half-dozen or so of the islands during the average seven day cruise. As on the previous day, today our itinerary called for visiting two islands in the course of a single morning and afternoon. The two islands were North Seymour and South Plaza. The wildlife on these islands were lucky in 1835 because Darwin had not visited either location and they were left in peace. The birds are tame ground-nesters and would have been easy pickings for a gun or a net and a gunnysack.

If a feral carnivore, or even a pair of omnivorous rats, ever gets loose on these small islands, the birds and land iguanas would be wiped out in a relatively short amount of time. Considering the large number of tourists continually visiting, arriving on ships with dark holds containing many nooks and crannies where stowaway rodents might hide, the continued existence of wildlife here depends on vigilant monitoring by the Park Service.

These two islands are close enough to the busy town of Puerto Ayora to attract day trippers as well as the groups like ours from the multi-day cruises, so the creatures here are subjected to an even greater degree of visitor impact than occurs on the more outlying islands.

The birds — ground nesting blue-footed boobies and bush nesting magnificent frigatebirds — seemed like they couldn't care less what anybody did. We stayed for only a short visit and to me it seemed irreverent to race through such an amazing wildlife spectacle in so short a period of time. Darwin had complained to Captain Fitzroy about getting rushed in various locations. In his journal he wrote, "It is the fate of most voyagers, no sooner to discover what is most interesting in any locality, than they are hurried from it."

When we left the islands we headed south, keeping the Santa Cruz coast about one mile to starboard as the *Angelique* cruised past first Punta Rocafuerte and then Punta Nunez.

Everyone returned to their cabins and gathered up gear. Soon the lights of Puerto Ayora appeared off the starboard bow as the captain took the *Angelique* into Academy Bay. In the darkness it was hard to tell that there was a bustling little town at the far end of the harbor.

Chapter Three
PUERTO AYORA

Dave McCargo and I intended staying in the Galapagos far longer than most visitors. On the first day of our arrival we checked into a hotel called *Los Amigos* in Puerto Ayora. This homey, hostel-like rooming house would become our base for the next five weeks. In 1996 28,000 people lived in the Galapagos, on the islands of Baltra, Santa Cruz, San Cristobal, Floreana and Isabela. 10,000 of those people live in Puerto Ayora.

In Darwin's time most of the Galapagos Islands had British names, many of those having been designated by pirate Ambrose Cowley in 1684. Ecuador annexed the islands in 1832 and they were eventually given

Spanish names. Santa Cruz, where Puerto Ayora is located, used to be called Indefatigable Island.

Boats anchored in the Academy Bay on Santa Cruz Island

One morning, I boarded one of the many colorful buses that leaves from near Puerto Ayora's dock and heads up into the lush highlands. I had the driver drop me off a half-hour later just south of the town of Santa Rosa at the beginning of a rural track leading into some farmland that a travel agency had told me was home to many of the giant tortoises for which the Galapagos are famous. It was 8:30 A.M. and there was thick morning fog. The humidity was so high, and there was so much dew, that when I walked under tree branches the moisture falling made it feel like it was raining.

A half-mile hike brought me to a lush pasture with about fifteen big, round lumps, each a giant tortoise, scattered over perhaps twenty acres. About eighty or so tortoises remain in the vicinity of the farmstead until April, at which time they migrate south to their nature reserve, named El Chato, to mate and lay eggs.

Two Galapagos tortoises in a faceoff display

I walked up a gradual incline to the upper end of the pasture. Just across a broken-down, barbed wire fence I saw two adult tortoises facing off, mouths wide open. It was more of a display than a fight, and one of the giant reptiles soon backed off and plodded slowly away.

The remaining tortoise became my next photo

subject. He was in thick vegetation with his head and neck protruding above some broad leaves. A vermilion flycatcher, one of the true darlings amongst Galapagos upland birdwatchers, momentarily landed on the tortoise's head. Unfortunately, he took off before I could set up the camera on my tripod and shoot.

Vermillion Flycatcher

I got up, hefted the tripod, and headed for the next tortoise. It was about 200 ft. away and looked like a shiny boulder. By now it was 3 P.M., sunny and very hot. All traces of the morning's rain and fog had disappeared.

On October 9, 1835, Darwin wrote in his diary that with the help of a guide he hiked to the "interior &

higher parts of the (Santiago) island." As was the case on Santa Cruz and other islands, the highlands of Santiago were more heavily vegetated than the lowlands. He estimated that he hiked eight miles that day to an elevation of about 3000 feet. He described "vapour condensed by the trees dripping down like rain" — the same phenomenon I had experienced earlier in the day before the fog lifted. The vegetation he encountered also sounded similar — "green & damp."

Darwin found a spring in the Santa Cruz highlands which attracted many giant tortoises. He notes in his diary that the tortoises are "so strong as easily to carry me, & too heavy to lift from the ground." He observed that "When they arrive at the Spring, they bury their heads above their eyes in the water &

Galapagos Tortoises in a pond on El Chato Tortoise Reserve

greedily suck in great mouthfuls, quite regardless of lookers on." He saw tortoise paths leading from all sides of the spring and extending for miles.

From the farmstead I walked back to the main road and in the process became thoroughly drenched in sweat. I felt as wet as if I had just gone for a swim.

I walked to the edge of the road and stuck out my thumb. I soon had a ride in the back of a panel truck. I stood up as we sped down the road, trying to capture every molecule of breeze that was available. As we approached a yellow and white farmhouse, the driver slowed down and came to a stop. An athletic-looking Galapadorean in his mid-twenties came running over and climbed into the back. He had a blue backpack draped over one shoulder and a noisy rooster under his other arm. The rooster gave out a *cock-a-doodle-doo* as we continued down the road.

We met many travelers passing through Puerto Ayora, in various stages of their journeys around the Galapagos Islands, around Ecuador and South America and, occasionally, around the world. Even though it is located on a remote island, Puerto Ayora is a crossroads and melting pot which scrambles people together from many walks of life and from many nations.

From the never-ending parade of people that I had the opportunity to speak with, by far the most bizarre story came from a young German law student named Inge Burke. The story actually was not about her, but dealt with a dog back in her native Germany.

It seems that the previous year, in Munich, an animal-loving housewife gave her miniature poodle a shampoo. She was in a hurry to have the animal's fur dry out, so she came up with the idea of putting the dog in her brand new microwave oven which she had owned for less than a week. The oven was the housewife's first microwave, and the instructions said nothing about dogs. It did, however, specify seven minutes for potatoes and four minutes for corn. She figured that three minutes couldn't hurt the dog. She placed the poodle inside, set the timer, and pressed ‘Start’. When the time was up and the buzzer sounded, she opened the door, looked inside, screamed, fainted, and had to be taken to the hospital. The dog was placed in a plastic bag and became the centerpiece of a liability lawsuit.

The housewife eventually sued the company that

had produced the microwave, claiming that they were negligent for not including an explicit warning against placing pets inside the appliance. The housewife won her case. As part of the settlement conditions in that lawsuit, all microwaves sold in Germany must now include the warning, "Unsafe For Live Animals." Darwin was often cruel in his experimentation with the native wildlife, such as when he condoned weighing down a marine iguana and trying to drown it. But at least his endeavors had a scientific motivation.

About eight-thirty each evening, Dave and I would head for one of the restaurants. Virtually all of the eating establishments were open-air and had ubiquitous mosquitoes Applying insect repellent became as second nature as putting on a pair of sandals. If you should forget the insect repellent, some of the restaurants provided it.

In one of the restaurants, we came across Juan Vera, our guide from the *Angelique.* As we ate, he entertained us with his repertoire of stories. We heard about the Swiss tourist who got lost for three weeks and drank tortoise blood to stay alive. And about a guide who touched a marine iguana on the snout and had his middle finger bitten completely off.

Juan went on, "There is a small, sweet-smelling fruit growing wild in the Galapagos that you don't want to eat. It is the poison apple, called *Manzanilla*. The tortoises can eat it, but you can't." As an afterthought he added, "Not more than once, that is. After all, we can eat anything once."

"There was a tourist ate three manzanilla apples and wound up in the hospital for five days. After that the tourist was nicknamed 'The Manzanilla Kid'. I later looked up the poison apple and found that it grows on the manchineel tree. It is a normal part of the diet of the giant tortoises.

In Darwin's journal I don't remember him mentioning this apple. He did, however, eat local island food.

On October 9th, 1835, while on his second of nine days camping on Santiago Island, he jotted down the following diary entry: "We lived on the meat of the Tortoise fried in transparent oil, which is procured from the fat. The breast-plate with the meat attached to it, is roasted. It is then very good. Young tortoises make capital soup; otherwise the meat is but — to my taste

— indifferent food."

When we had all finished our meals and drinks, Juan mentioned the fifteen inch centipede. "There are over 1600 species of insects in the Galapagos Islands," he said, "but only one can kill you."

Actually, I already knew about this Godzilla centipede, *Scolopendra galapagensis.* There were eight native species of centipedes in the Galapagos. Technically it was not really an insect, but was a member of the arthropod family. And while it was true that it occasionally catches and kills birds and small reptiles, I had never heard of any human dying from its bite. Furthermore, after weeks of hiking around on the islands I had not seen even one of these behemoths. I mentioned this to Juan.

"It only takes one encounter to be convinced ," Juan assured me. "It comes in the night, when you're least expecting it."

Chapter Four
SIERRA NEGRA

"Many creatures hence may see the Galapagos as thickly inhabited by the human species as any other part of the world. At present, they are only fit for tortoises, iguanas, lizards, snakes, etc."

Captain David Porter

Aboard the U.S. Frigate Essex

James Bay, Isla Santiago, Galapagos

August 1813

I had already sampled many of the experiences of the Galapagos during the past three weeks. That time period was only two weeks short of the total amount of time that Darwin himself had spent here. I had visited the islands of Fernandina, Floreana, Isabela, Santiago,

Bartolome, North Seymour, and South Plaza. This was accomplished at seven knots and under partial-sail aboard the *Angelique.* In addition I had been on Baltra and Santa Cruz. Nine islands.

Now I was interested in exploring Sierra Negra, one of the six high volcanoes on Isabela Island. Darwin had not had the opportunity to climb any of that island's volcanoes. Captain Fitzroy was mainly interested in surveying and mapping the islands and every other activity received lower priority. Darwin expressed some frustration at this state of affairs but the matter was out of his control. He had the unpaid position of ship's geologist and naturalist and was not involved in any voyage decision making. The fact that Darwin did not get to visit the top of any of the volcanoes made me even more determined to reach at least one summit.

Sierra Negra, at 4890 feet, is the third highest volcano on Isabela after *Volcan Wolf* and *Cerro Azul.* From north to south it is the fourth volcano in line.

From Puerto Ayora we took a municipal transport boat, the *Estrella del Mar*, and cruised for five hours to the tiny port town of Puerto Villamil on the southeast coast of Isabela. The *Estrella del Mar* is about forty feet long and is the twice weekly "bus service" between the two islands. Sixty or so passengers sprawl all over the upper and lower decks while in transit.

During the passage I met a national park service guide named Antonio Gil and explained that we wanted to camp on the rim of Sierra Negra Volcano. He told us we could join a horseback trip he had arranged to go up there two days hence.

From a distance, *Sierra Negra* doesn't look like much of a mountain. Although nearly a mile high, its slopes ascend so gradually that one is left with the impression that one is merely looking at a wide, low hill. This appearance is typical of basaltic shield volcanoes, of which Sierra Negra is one. Mauna Loa, a better known shield volcano in Hawaii, is about two and a half miles high, yet still gives the impression of being no more than a very wide hill.

Sierra Negra's appearance is deceptive. A mile is high and steep, regardless of how benign the incline of a slope may seem. The first leg of the transport up its slopes, in an old, rickety bus, was very taxing on the vehicle. We frequently smelled burning rubber and an overheating engine, requiring several rest stops during the forty-minute ride.

At just after 7 A.M. we arrived at a little shack with saddled horses and a wrangler nearby. We had 150 pounds of camping gear with us consisting of two 50 pound backpacks plus six gallons of water. We tied our gear onto the two horses and walked behind them.

The wrangler and horses were soon way ahead of us and out of sight. We plodded up the slopes slowly. Cattle were scattered about and at one point we encountered a Brahma-type bull with long horns at close enough range to be able to observe eye movement. About an hour into our march we crested the rim of the volcano. The enormous panorama of Sierra Negra's caldera opened before us. The view took my breath away. It is a shame that this was a sight that Darwin had never seen.

The fairly symmetrical caldera has 300 ft. walls. It is six miles long by four and a half miles wide, making it the second largest caldera in the world, after Tanzania's famed *NgoroNgoro Crater*. But while the latter is in a geologically stable region, unlikely to explode any time in the near future, Sierra Negra is relatively young --less than one million years old --with a subterranean environment that is active, smoldering and possesses the very real potential for erupting anew at any time.

Cerro Azul, Sierra Negra's sister volcano to the south, put on a fireworks display in 1979 with a dramatic eruption. It erupted again in 1999, an event prompting the airlifting of tortoises from its slopes for transport to safety at the Puerto Villamil tortoise rearing center. The two volcanoes have similar plumbing, and one could go off just as readily as the other. Sierra Negra has had ten documented eruptions between 1813 and 1979.

On November 13, 1979 at 7:30 A.M. an earthquake occurred on Isabela Island. At 8 A.M. a second earthquake struck. Forty-five minutes after that an explosion was heard by ranchers near the southeastern slope of *Sierra Negra*. There is a vent on that outer slope called *Volcan Chico*, and from that vent spewed an eruptive cloud large enough to be seen by the National Oceanic and Atmospheric Administration's SMS-I weather satellite. Lava shot three hundred feet into the air. Twenty active vents opened, and lava poured out forming thirteen separate flows. Much of the lava from those flows reached the ocean, where it raised the water temperature *eighteen miles* from shore.

While some pioneering vegetation has taken root in the black lava of the crater's floor, much of this otherworldly landscape remains barren of greenery, indicating the recent eruption activity. It is easy to look down from the rim and imagine a lake of red molten lava bubbling up from the depths, a lake so hot and so vast that the air temperature would be instantly lethal.

The *Volcan Chico* eruption in 1979 was not related to the formation of the caldera. *Chico's* eruption was only a minor event in *Sierra Negra's* history. The caldera itself formed when a previous enormous eruption finally ceased, and the lava lake gradually cooled and subsided. It dropped ultimately to its current position three hundred feet below the level of the rim.

This entire process --eruption, lava lake, subsidence, caldera formation- - could repeat itself at any moment. Molten magma is currently present below the caldera at a depth of less than two miles.

As I looked across the vast bowl, I was well aware of these dynamics of a landscape that is still very much alive. It's an exciting, if unsettling, notion that there is no *terra firma* here. The very land I was standing on was in a state of flux, and there was no guarantee it would remain the same from one day to the next.

The Sierra Negra caldera, with 300 ft. high walls

I took many photographs of the changing scene as we skirted the caldera's rim. The sky was a clear, deep blue and the morning sun very bright. I imagined Darwin aboard the *Beagle* gazing up from nearly a mile below us and additional miles off to the northwest, probably wishing that he could be up here.

After about an hour-and-a-half, we caught up with the wrangler and horses in a small clearing along Sierra Negra's northeastern ridge. We went a quarter-mile farther and unloaded our gear under an enormous tree.

When Darwin visited Isabela in October of 1835, five of the main volcanoes each had a healthy population of its own distinct race of Galapagos tortoise. These were five of the original fourteen subspecies of giant tortoises.

Today the same five subspecies still exist on Isabela, but only *Alcedo*, the next volcano to the north of *Sierra Negra*, contains what can be thought of as a robust population. 36% of all tortoises in the Galapagos are found on *Alcedo*. Time has not been so kind to the other four races.

The reason for the decline in populations, historically, has been decimation by pirates and whalers, who loaded tortoises by the hundreds aboard their ships to provide a ready meat supply. The unfortunate animals, stacked one atop the other below deck, would remain alive for many months without food or water. Each large tortoise provided about two hundred pounds of meat. Overall, it is estimated that between 100,000 and 200,000 tortoises were killed. Between 1811 and 1844 alone, more than fifteen thousand tortoises were removed from the islands for food. That number approximately equals the total number of giant tortoises remaining alive today. Darwin's ship was an active participant in this harvest: the *Beagle* took forty-eight tortoises aboard, plus the three baby tortoises that Darwin personally brought back to England alive.

In his diary entry for September 17th, 1835, two days after making landfall on San Cristobal Island, Darwin wrote that "the Tortoise is so abundant that a single Ship's company here caught 500-800 in a short time."

But even by 1835, the tortoise numbers in the Galapagos had been greatly reduced. When on Floreana Island, Darwin wrote in his diary entry for September 24th that the main article of animal food for the 250 permanent human residents was the tortoise. He indicated that two days of hunting would provide meat for everyone for a full week, but that the tortoise numbers had declined in recent years. He mentioned that not many years before his visit "the Ship's company of a Frigate brought down to the Beach in one day more than 200." He went on to say that where the springs are on Floreana the tortoises "formerly swarmed." When Darwin spoke with the island's governor, Nicholas Lawson, he was told that there were enough tortoises left to feed the settlement for only another twenty years.

Today the greatest threat to the remaining tortoises comes from the introduction of feral animals–mainly black rats, goats, dogs, and pigs. The rats, dogs, and pigs eat the eggs and young hatchlings. Feral goats overgraze the land, consuming vegetation that tortoises depend upon for their survival.

The *Sierra Negra* subspecies of the tortoise population is in such critical danger of extinction that officials have collected all members of this subspecies that they could find and taken them to a tortoise-rearing facility just outside of Puerto Villamil. Within a year of the establishment of the facility in 1995, about seventy tortoises of varying ages had been collected and were being cared for in the rearing pens. Hopefully, some day they can be returned to the wild with the confidence that they will survive. Their fate depends upon the long term efficacy of the feral animal eradication program.

The decline of the tortoise numbers is unfortunate, and one of the sad legacies of human contact with this most special of archipelagos. On three other islands in the Galapagos, the giant tortoises have fared even worse. Three subspecies–one per island–have gone extinct. A fourth subspecies, from the island of Pinta, has only one remaining representative, and therefore his kind is inevitably doomed to extinction as well (unless he is cloned, which scientists have considered).

The wrangler departed with his horses, and Dave and I put up our tents under the larger of two giant shade trees. We then set out, each of us in a different direction, to investigate the bizarre landscape.

The floor of Sierra Negra's caldera, three hundred feet below me, was not readily accessed from our camp area, so I chose to walk along the outer, northeastern flank of this temporarily dormant volcano. After twenty minutes of walking through some thin brush, I stepped out into a scene as foreign looking as if I had just set foot on another planet.

The land looked tortured. Bare black lava lay twisted and jumbled for miles. You could see where it had, in times past, poured over the lip of the volcano and flowed in a northeasterly direction. As it flowed it had piled up on itself, creating weird and fantastic formations as some parts of the molten river cooled and slowed before others.

Most of the lava was the rough *aa* type, mixed with basalt. This is the most common type of lava found on earth. But also evident was a small area of *pahoehoe*, the kind we had seen on Santiago Island near Sullivan Bay. Unlike the flow of pahoehoe, aa lava tumbles along as it is formed, creating very sharp, jagged edges.

Throughout the vastness of this primeval panorama were random small volcanic cones by the dozens, sticking up like miniature *Mt. St. Helens'*, all with their tops blown off. I climbed several of these. When I peered over their tops I discovered scaled-down calderas, little versions of *Sierra Negra's* gargantuan bowl.

Not all of the lava was black. Certain of the cones appeared to have been partially painted with whites and yellows. I climbed around these areas and was hit in the face by sulphur-smelling steam coming out of active vents. The ground was alive as I scrambled over it. Deep underneath, molten lava boiled any surface water that managed to seep far enough down into the earth to make contact. The water then evaporated and rose to the surface again, breaking out into the atmosphere in the form of hot, sulfurous steam through openings called *fumaroles*.

This northeast slope of *Sierra Negra* was full of them. In my random scrambling around, I found three that were over sixty feet across and very deep. The hot, moist, shady environments inside the larger fumaroles provide microclimates suitable to ferns. By inching over to the edges of the precipices on my belly and peeking down inside the hollow vents, I discovered hidden and unlikely picturesque little vegetated grottos tucked into this otherwise stark landscape.

In some areas the ground itself was steaming, right up through the volcanic cinder. Such a sight was even more eerie than the steaming vents. It gave me the feeling that the ground itself was on fire and about to explode at any moment. Of course, on this island, that was always a real possibility.

Having the opportunity of encountering these phenomena by oneself instead of in a group adds to the sense of drama and intensifies the experience. To be surrounded by miles and miles of a rough, black, otherworldly tapestry, and to see the very earth beneath your feet spewing forth its hot, dragon-like breath, lets one's imagination run wild.

From my position about three-quarters of a mile down the outer slope of Sierra Negra, where *Volcan Chico* is located below the rim, I climbed back up to the top. I arrived just in time to catch a glimpse of the sun setting into a low cloud bank on the far side of the caldera. Ever-changing shadows worked their way across the crater's high walls and floor. And, as is the case on the equator everywhere in the world, dusk descended rapidly. I didn't waste any time in finding my way back to camp.

Although Darwin never had the opportunity to explore the high crater rims on Isabela, he did make many observations of the island's general volcanic features from his vantage point below. He first stepped foot on the island on September 29th and wrote that 'the Volcanic origin of all is but too plainly evident." Whatever lower elevation craters he was able to see he referred to as "very perfect and generally red-coloured within." The following day, on September 30th, he noticed "steam issuing from a crater." Darwin knew already, from journals written by others a decade earlier, that active volcanism was to be expected in the islands. The H.M.S. Blonde made the discovery on that ship's visit to the archipelago. An entry by one of the *Blonde's* crewmates for March 27, 1825 said, "About half way down the steep southeast side of Narborough (Fernandina) Island, a volcano burns day and night, and near the beach a crater was pouring forth streams of lava, which on reaching the sea caused it to bubble in an extraordinary manner."

Although Darwin didn't climb the major volcanoes, he must have reached a satisfactory viewpoint in order to have made some of his observations, particularly an entry in his diary on October 1, 1835 when he wrote: "...from the mountain behind, great bare streams have flowed, sometimes from the summit, or from small Craters on the side, expanding in their descent, have at the base formed plains of Lava."

The following morning I was startled awake at 4 A.M. by the raucous braying of a feral burro about two feet from my ear, just on the outer side of the tent's mosquito netting. At 5:30 a riot of bird sounds announced the coming of dawn.

I dressed rapidly, grabbed a small daypack with camera, film and cookies, and headed up the trail to watch the sunrise on the crater's rim. A thick fog enshrouded everything. The fog plus the cool, damp morning air made me feel for the moment more like I was in some Oregon coastal region than in the equatorial tropics.

Visibility was about fifty feet in the fog. The trail along the volcano's rim was very narrow, and small spiders had strung their webs across it by the thousands. After a few face- and mouthfuls of spider webs, I learned to hike while holding a stick vertically out in front of me at arm's length. The webs I walked through probably represented hundreds, if not thousands, of total spider-hours of labor. I regretted destroying all those spiders' handiwork, but the circumstances allowed me no other reasonable alternative.

I broke out of the vegetation along the tangled trail onto a clearing of lava in time to see a muted sun rise through a surprise thinning of the shifting fog. Minutes later the fog thickened again, swallowing the yellow globe.

During brief partial clearings I could make out the narrow waist of Isabela Island far below to the north. The large concavity of Elizabeth Bay could be seen to the west of the isthmus. Santa Cruz and Santiago Islands were offshore to the east. *Alcedo* Volcano rose gradually, in typical shield fashion, just beyond Elizabeth Bay, with *Darwin* Volcano poking its head up just past *Alcedo*. The most northerly and highest volcano, *Wolf*, could not be seen.

In the cool morning temperature, the sulfurous volcanic steam rose in long, wispy plumes from the many active fumaroles on the eastern slope below me. The panorama seemed like the perfect stage for prehistoric creatures to walk across.

I was only able to enjoy brief glimpses of this stunning spectacle. The prevailing southeasterly winds, which were moderate in strength but relentless, brought in wave after wave of fog. It rose up the volcano's outer slopes and flowed over the lip and across the enormous maw, enshrouding the caldera.

I lingered in the fog for some two hours hoping it would lift, and then returned to our campsite. It wasn't until noon that the fog cleared entirely.

At the end of the day we returned to the crater rim to catch another sunset. We heard squawking as a pair of the endemic Galapagos hawks glided gracefully by, one hundred feet below us. I don't know what they were hunting. In two days on the rim I had only seen lava lizards, burros, a few butterflies and spiders, aside from an assortment of diminutive song birds. Perhaps they were after the endemic rice rat, or the introduced black and Norway rats. The hawks looked like a smaller version of the Northern Hemisphere's golden eagle.

Darwin first mentions seeing a hawk when he was on San Cristobal Island on September 17, 1835. While my own interest was in the beauty of the landscape and the wildlife, Darwin's focus, as always, was that of the specimen collector and scientific observer. He wrote in his diary, "Little birds within 3 or four feet, quietly hopped about the Bushes & were not frightened by stones thrown at them. I pushed off a branch with the end of my gun a large Hawk." He later referred to these hawks as "carrion-buzzards."

Galapagos Hawk

The next morning, after the fog had lifted, I could see to the north the vast lava barrier between Sierra

Negra and Alcedo Volcano. The lava field was about 15 miles long by 10 miles wide. While burros and goats might negotiate this expanse, the giant tortoises cannot. I could easily grasp how each of the volcanoes on Isabela is really a biological island unto itself, at least as far as tortoises are concerned. Each volcano has its own giant tortoise subspecies which has no chance of ever visiting an adjacent volcano.

Eons ago, when this island was fully vegetated, the common ancestor to the Galapagos tortoise probably hopped on a debris raft and made a serendipitous journey over from the mainland. Perhaps one pair made the journey, or perhaps a number of pairs arrived intact. They reproduced and spread out. With vegetation everywhere, there was little limitation to their movements. They inhabited the entire island.

The various volcanoes eventually erupted and life changed for the tortoises. Lava rivers flowed and killed all plant life in their paths. Dried lava fields became an effective migration barrier and each volcano became biologically isolated from its neighbors. As far as the wholly terrestrial giant tortoise was concerned, the isolation was as effective and absolute as if there was ocean rather than lava separating the five volcanoes.

Subsequently, over thousands of years, the originally similar populations each diverged from the others. Each developed its own characteristics in response to the unique challenges presented to it by the environment of its home volcano.

Lava barriers were easy to comprehend. Not so easy to understand were some other evolutionary twists, such as why in all the Galapagos Archipelago had cormorants lost their ability to fly only in the relatively limited area we could now view below us, stretching from Elizabeth Bay to Fernandina Island to Punta Albemarle. Why aren't these vestigial-winged seabirds found on all the other islands as well? The answer to this puzzle is not to be found even within the scope of Darwin's teachings.

As the time approached 4 P.M., we headed back across the lava fields to the crater's rim above camp. We arrived at the top in time for sundown. The caldera looked like a witch's giant cauldron as fog poured eerily over the eastern lip, running right over our heads and hanging suspended across the wide expanse.

By the time we returned to our tents, the fog entirely

enveloped us, reducing visibility to sixty or seventy feet.

The following morning we packed up and broke camp, put on our backpacks, and hiked the three miles out to the road. From there we were able to hitch a ride in an open truck down off the volcano's slopes and back to Puerto Villamil.

Not far out of town along the beach were dozens of tracks that had been made by sea turtles the night before. I came across two large turtles that were just beginning the arduous task of hauling themselves out of the ocean and across the sand to above the high tide line. There they would eventually excavate a pit and lay their eggs. The entire process, from leaving the water until they return back into the sea, usually takes three to four hours, even though the distance covered is barely three hundred feet.

When I returned to our room in Antonio Gil's hotel, I told David about the turtles. After dinner, about 10 PM, we walked back down to the beach.

Of the world's sea turtles, all of which are endangered, only the Pacific green sea turtle nests in the Galapagos. As the turtle emerges from the ocean on to the beach sand, she makes a set of tracks about two-

and-a-half feet wide which appears very much like the pattern a miniature caterpillar-driven vehicle might make.

It's excruciating to watch one of these big 200 pound turtles trudge laboriously up on to the beach. The female hauls herself out of the surf, drags herself a few feet forward on the sand, then seems exhausted by the effort and hangs her head and rests. Then she crawls forward again a few feet, rests, crawls forward, rests...

As we walked along the dark beach we came across a fresh set of tracks. We followed them to above the high tide line but found nothing. The same was the case with the next two sets of tracks we discovered. The fourth set of tracks led us up to a four-foot-wide crater, positioned well beyond the high tide line. In it was a large sea turtle, her head and back covered with sand. She was using both her front and back flippers to deepen the pit that she was in. When I stood behind her in the darkness, I was hit by flying sand. The digging process was very slow. Sand would fly for about thirty seconds, followed by a pause, then another burst of digging, then another pause. Again and again.

By following tracks, we discovered three other nesting females, all of whom were in the process of excavation. None had yet laid their usual eighty or so eggs. Each turtle will repeat this process about eight times during the nesting season, laying a total of perhaps six hundred eggs. Of these, approximately five percent survive. Until humans came upon the scene in the last two hundred years, a five percent survival rate was adequate to provide for perpetuation of the species.

Beetles, ghost crabs, sharks, and herons account for most of the natural mortality of sea turtle eggs and hatchlings. It is a fragile system, but for millennia it has maintained a successful turtle population.

Chapter Five
EL CHATO

We returned to Puerto Ayora by boat early the next day. The time we had spent in the Galapagos was now just one week shy of the five weeks that Darwin spent here in 1835.

I decided to return one more time to the *El Chato* Tortoise Reserve in the Santa Cruz highlands. I had been there a week-and-a-half ago and wanted to observe the giant tortoises in the wild again. Like *Sierra Negra* Volcano, the Tortoise Reserve is one of the few wild places in the Galapagos that can be visited without a national park guide. It's free and requires only a willingness to hike.

The next morning I caught the 6:30 AM bus out of

Puerto Ayora. There is only one main road on the island, and the bus takes it up into the highlands, dropping off locals at various homesteads along the way. I got off the bus at Santa Rosa and met a Swiss couple who were looking for the Tortoise Reserve. I mentioned to them that it was possible to rent horses to carry them into the reserve and they went up to a small, nearby dwelling to inquire about rentals. I preferred to walk so that I could take time to photograph, and I went directly to the trailhead at the edge of the woods.

Due to the fact that two tourists had gotten lost in the reserve in the past few years, there were posted at the trailhead a plethora of warnings.

Santa Cruz Island covers 379 square miles, and the Tortoise Reserve occupies about a sixth of that area. It is located in the extreme southwestern portion of the island, stretching from the coast inland.

The trail into the reserve is a poorly maintained path that sometimes requires a bit of imagination to stay on. But for most of the route it follows the fence line of adjacent ranchland. The tortoises, of course, don't know parkland from private land, and can be found on either side of the barbed wire fence.

A Galapagos tortoise can weigh 800 pounds

At one point I sat down right next to the fence to watch a female tortoise that was grazing nearby. Soon a big male tortoise (males can be told from females by their size, being much larger) came crunching his way through the dense foliage and headed right for the female --who then headed right toward me. I held my ground and watched, as seven hundred pounds of reptiles came my way.

When motivated — such as by the mating urge — these creatures move a lot faster than one would ever expect. In his diary on October 9, 1835, Darwin wrote that he thought the tortoises could "march at a rate of 360 yards in an hour; perhaps 4 miles in the 24." He based this estimate on observations of tortoises coming and going to a watering hole on Santiago Island.

At the last possible moment the pair veered slightly to my right, walking over my backpack, and going right under the bottom strand of the tightly strung barbed wire. Fortunately, there was nothing in the backpack that could be harmed by these reptilian steam rollers.

Half-way down the 3.5 mile trail, in a small picturesque, shaded grove, was a large gray wooden sign. The story behind the sign has become legendary on Santa Cruz Island. The sign read:

> "In memory of Guy Nachmoni,
> from Israel, only 23 years old,
> who disappeared on this island,
> in the tortoise reserve, on the
> 9th of July, 1991."

The event traumatized the island community.

The sign was erected in November 1991, four months after Nachmoni's disappearance. Just one month after the dedication of the sign, Guy Nachmoni's body was discovered, well off the trail, part-way towards the ocean. The circumstances surrounding his death still remain a mystery.

A Swiss tourist was lost on the reserve in 1993. For three weeks he could not find his way out. He was resourceful, though, and, as Juan Vera had already related, he managed to survive the dehydrating heat by subsisting on tortoise blood.

Memorial sign for Guy Nachmoni in El Chato Tortoise Reserve

I was visiting in the rainy season (January through June), so the hiking milieu was a little more forgiving. Guavas and passion fruits then grow in abundance along the trail, so I was able to keep happily fed and hydrated as I trekked along. Nachmoni visited in July which was the beginning of the five-month dry season. It may have been a fraction cooler in that season, but the lack of water here can be deadly, to man and reptile alike.

Past the Nachmoni memorial are stands of forest draped with club moss, giving the land a fairytale appearance. It is like a miniature version of Olympic National Park's Hoh Rainforest, in the state of Washington.

I heard loud grunting coming from some bushes so I maneuvered my way through thick vegetation to discover a pair of mating tortoises. The male was propped up awkwardly on the back of the female. The clever adaptation making these calisthenics possible is the concave shape of the male's bottom shell, the plastron. While the fit to the female's upper shell, her carapace, is not exactly like a glove, it is adequate to get the job done. I took a few x-rated photos, then left the pair to continue with their somewhat less than delicate logistics.

At the end of the trail was a muddy pond beneath *El Chato* Hill. A less distinct trail actually goes further on, but most hikers do not venture beyond this point. By the time I reached the pond I was drenched in sweat. My shirt and pants were ringing wet.

El Chato pond had dried to half the size of what it

was when I had visited it the previous week. If it didn't rain soon (this was an exceedingly dry rainy season), the wildlife would suffer. Galapagos tortoises typically spend long parts of their days partially submerged in ponds. White-cheeked pintail ducks also depend on the water, as do gallinules, which are long-toed water birds that are members of the rail family. Watering holes in this part of the world are very scarce, and the few that there are on Santa Cruz are used thirstily by domestic livestock as well as by wildlife.

Darwin commented on the precarious water situation in the Galapagos. On September 23, 1835, when on Floreana Island, he wrote, "The main evil under which these islands suffer is the scarcity of water." He notes that Pacific islands in general "are subject to years of drought & subsequent scarcity," and that "I should be

afraid this group (the Galapagos Islands) will not afford an exception."

Today we know that wet and dry periods are part of the rhythm of life in the Galapagos and can be explained by the El Nino-La Nina phenomenon. During El Ninos, which occur every 2-9 years, the ocean becomes warmer and atmospheric changes occur favoring more rainfall. The opposite takes place during *La Ninas*, which are accompanied by severe drought. The most severe El Nino recorded in the Galapagos was in 1982-83 and the second greatest was 1997-98. Each El Nino is followed by a *La Nina.* A *La Nina* was experienced in the Galapagos shortly before my trip to the islands.

After photographing at the pond, I began the hot walk back. Along the way I counted eleven giant tortoises, plus about four times that many cows, horses, and other assorted farm animals.

While hiking out, the fence line between private land and the tortoise reserve was on my left side. I noticed a tortoise way out in a field on the private side of the fence. I took off my pack, pushed it under the lowest strand of barbed wire, and then by carefully spreading the two bottom strands, I climbed through. I put my pack back on and hiked over to the tortoise, which turned out to be an ex-tortoise. It was the very large and complete shell --carapace plus plastron- -of what had been an old male.

The shell wasn't bleached out, so I assumed the tortoise hadn't been dead for too many years. Being as big as he was, perhaps he was a hundred years old when he died. There is no way to accurately age a tortoise by its shell, so the age of the remains was anybody's guess. Darwin wrote in his diary on September 24, 1835 that Governor Lawson of Floreana Island had informed him that a tortoise was captured in 1830 which had various dates carved on its shell, including one that was from 1786. The tortoise was so big that it required ten men to lift it into the boat.

I hiked the three and a half miles back to the road. By the time the bus arrived, a heavy, pounding rain had begun. The rain was desperately needed. It cooled things down instantly. It would refill *El Chato* Pond and would top off the few smaller watering holes. The pintails, gallinules and tortoises would be granted a reprieve for the moment.

Chapter Six
BLUE FOOTED BOOBIES

Like many visitors to the Galapagos, I fell under the spell of the comical blue-footed booby. The name itself conjures up the notion of an imbecile, and the Spanish derivation of the word does, indeed, mean "dunce".

During a standard seven-day Galapagos cruise, most tourists get to walk briefly through a blue-footed booby colony on either Espanola or North Seymour Island. Weeks ago, on our boat journey, we spent about one and a half hours on North Seymour, with perhaps a third of those ninety minutes in the booby colony itself. That encounter was too short and served only to whet my appetite. I became hopelessly fascinated with the birds and their outrageous antics. So in my fifth week on the islands, after the *Angelique* cruise and after the *Sierra Negra* and *El Chato* hiking experiences, I was determined to revisit North Seymour.

Darwin never visited North Seymour or any of the blue-footed booby colonies. He makes no mention in his journals of having encountered the species at all. He writes about having observed and collected twenty-six kinds of "land" birds and eleven kinds of waders and water birds but he does not identify any bird corresponding to the blue-footed booby.

Mating dance of the blue-footed booby

I hired James Domingo and his twenty-four foot speedboat, *North Star*, for a day's outing. James, a certified Galapagos National Park guide, was well-versed in the natural history of the islands, and reasonably bilingual. Until 1996, he guided for packaged tours aboard commercial yachts and sailboats. He then decided to become more of an entrepreneur, so he bought his own boat and started taking groups out on day trips to the closer islands and dive sites. The *North Star* could reach North Seymour Island from Puerto Ayora in one hour and forty-five minutes. We worked out the arrangements on a Friday evening. He said I should be at the dock at 7 o'clock sharp the next morning.

There are three species of boobies in the Galapagos–the blue-footed, the red-footed, and the masked. Of these, the blue-footed, *Sula nebouxi*, is the most well-known. This is because of the eye-popping intense blue color of the bird's feet, and its irresistibly engaging courtship behavior. The blue-footed booby appears as a commercial Galapagos logo more than any other bird species in the islands. It appears ubiquitously on T-shirts in all the local shops. There is a "Blue-footed Construction Company", and a "Hotel Booby". There is booby-this and booby-that. This bird is the Galapagos' most showcased species of wildlife after the giant tortoise. I feel certain that Darwin must have at least seen a few of this species, although I could not find mention of it in his writings.

Of the seventy thousand blue-footed boobies in the world, thirty percent live in the Galapagos Islands. Red-footed boobies are much more common, with five hundred thousand resident birds. There are eighty thousand masked boobies here.

Dave McCargo and I arrived at the loading dock at 6:45 in the morning and were soon underway. By 8 AM the sun was already high and hot. The seas were smooth and we raced north. Without slowing, we passed through a large group of dolphins, many of which came over to swim alongside the boat. They were easily able to keep pace with our fast outboard motor, even when we were cranked up to full speed. One dolphin had a calf with it, and even the small calf was able to maintain our speed in seemingly effortless fashion. Hundreds of slim flying fish jumped across our path as we sped through the water.

When I spotted a humpback whale a quarter-mile off the starboard side, we slowed way down and eased the boat in the direction of the great creature. Only the top of its back, and occasionally the tail fluke, showed above the surface. The whale seemed neither interested in nor particularly afraid of our boat. He bobbed at the surface comfortably and lazily. In 1986, the sea surrounding the islands was added to the land masses in officially being offered protection with the establishment of the Galapagos Marine Reserve. In 1990, the area received the additional designation of Galapagos Whale Sanctuary. In Darwin's time, many whaling boats plied these waters and there is frequent mention of them in his diary.

The humpback slowly cruised the surface for a while before finally raising its tail, sounding, and disappearing from sight. As soon as the whale had vanished, we throttled up and quickly resumed top speed. We pulled up to the coast of North Seymour Island at 9:30.

We started up the trail, which was carefully marked by short wooden posts. All tour paths on all of the islands are meticulously designated. Straying off the trail is not permitted. Some Park Service guides are a little more lenient in this regard than others, but by and large the rule is adhered to.

Such strict regulation is necessary on the islands due

to the burgeoning volume of tourism. Over 150,000 tourists visit the islands each year. Unregulated visitation would quickly create havoc and alter or destroy the various natural phenomena that people come such long distances to experience. Mandatory accompaniment by guides and regulated travel are the logical solutions to dealing with the enormous tourist influx.

Even with the human race behaving itself in the Galapagos, nature can still dish out some nasty blows. When *El Nino* strikes, the ocean waters around the Galapagos warm up with the result that fewer fish survive. Consequently the seabirds, such as the boobies, have a tough time feeding their offspring and themselves. Man seems to get blamed for all disasters that befall wildlife. We are usually the most obvious and convenient whipping post. But in the Spring of 1983, when the most extraordinary *El Nino* on record struck the eastern Pacific Ocean, the simultaneous disappearance of the famed blue-footed booby colony on the Galapagos' Espanola Island could in no way be attributed to tourist impact. Fortunately, the birds later returned.

Male magnificent frigatebird displaying gular sac on North Seymour Island

North Seymour is a tiny, low island, barely 0.8 square miles in size. It has a three-quarter mile circular trail leading through large colonies of blue-footed boobies and magnificent frigatebirds. The latter are famous for the male's dramatic red throat pouch, called a "gular sac", which can be inflated to an enormous size in an attempt to attract females. But it is the blue-footed booby which is the real tourist charmer.

Of the three species of boobies in the Galapagos, the masked variety is the largest. The blue-footed booby, the mid-sized of this trio, is 2.5 feet long, with a wingspan of 5 feet. They have yellow eyes, and as is true with some species of eagles, the female is larger than the male. There is little competition for food amongst the booby species: the red-footed feeds far out at sea, while the blue footed feeds close to shore. They eat mainly fish-- anchovies, sardines, mackerel and flying fish, and occasionally squid. They catch their prey by plunge diving from heights of up to 300 feet, hitting the water at 60 mph and reaching depths of 82 ft. Males generally fish at shallower depths than females. Both sexes have permanently closed nostrils, a specialized feature for diving. They breathe instead through the corners of their mouths.

When Dave and I, aboard the *Angelique*, had visited this island nearly three weeks previously, many dozens of blue-footed booby pairs were comically engaged in their outrageous courtship displays–the females honked, the males whistled, and both sexes took part in sky-pointing (head, neck and beak straight up), waddling with slow motion foot-raising, and ultimately in mounting and mating.

By our second visit things had changed.

The boobies were now three weeks further into their nesting season. Most displaying had ceased. Instead of seeing lively courting and dancing pairs, we came upon blue-foots sitting on eggs which had been laid in the intervening weeks. The eggs were approximately chicken size, and each bird sat on from one to three of them. The vaudeville courtships had obviously been a great success.

The "nest" of the blue-footed booby consists of just a patch of bare ground. Although the boobies do not build a nest structure, both parents certainly pay close attention to their eggs. In the relentless Galapagos sun, it is not so much a matter of keeping the eggs warm as it is of keeping them cool, at least during the intense midday heat. The parent in attendance keeps the eggs in continual shade by sitting on or hovering over them, with his or her back always to the sun. The birds look

Nesting blue-footed booby providing shade for eggs

miserable and tortured in the heat, but they faithfully attend to their task.

The incubation period for blue-footed booby eggs is about 41-45 days. It would be several more weeks before the cute white chicks would emerge, and I regretted that I wouldn't be present for the event. One really needs to live in the Galapagos year 'round in order to comprehend the complete life cycle of these birds. Darwin, during his five week visit, only obtained a short snapshot of the life cycle of the archipelago's wildlife.

Although many of the boobies were currently protecting two or three eggs, the survival of more than a single chick is uncertain at best. It would depend on how plentiful a year it was for the food supply. If the parents could catch enough fish, two chicks *might* survive. It would be very rare to have all three make it. In lean years it is a matter of survival of the fittest, with the weakest one or two chicks starving to death. The chicks feed off regurgitated fish in the adult's mouth. If the parent does not have enough food for all the chicks, it will only feed the biggest one. In this manner only the strongest get to survive and thus to pass on their DNA to the next generation.

I finished up photographing for the day and we returned to the boat. The engine was started and we headed south. We were now going against the tide and the boat bounced like crazy.

We first skirted along the east coast of Baltra, and then continued down along the coast of Santa Cruz Island, passing between it and the land iguana havens of North and South Plaza Islands, which were a little further to the east.

Chapter Seven
KAYAKING AT PUNTA ESTRADA

During my visit in 1996, individual freelance kayaking was not one of the enterprises that had blossomed accompanying the influx of tourists to the Galapagos Islands. After some searching I discovered that Polo and Monica Navarro, the owners of the *Red Mangrove* Inn in Puerto Ayora, had a rack of *Seda* fiberglass kayaks for rent. "Not many people go kayaking," lamented Polo, who invested many thousands of dollars purchasing his rental crafts. "I would like to go on a kayak expedition myself, but I don't have time. Now, in March, is the best time of year to paddle all around the island."

Darwin had little time for leisure activities during his

busy weeks in the Galapagos. Virtually all his energies were devoted to surveying harbors and land forms and collecting a myriad of wildlife and plant specimens. He seemed to detest sailing and being aboard a vessel on the sea. He certainly did not spend any more time in boats than was absolutely necessary. I'm sure the notion of kayaking would have been abhorrent to him. During the five year voyage of the *Beagle*, Darwin spent two-thirds of his time on shore and would have spent even more time on land if Captain Fitzroy had allowed it.

I chose a sleek, red kayak from the rack located on the small private dock behind Polo and Monica's inn. Polo helped me get the boat down and ease it into the water.

While leaving the shallows I encountered a huge great blue heron, standing over three feet tall. Great blues are by far the largest herons in the Galapagos. Only reluctantly did he get out of my way.

It was 10 AM and the sun had already been intense for three hours. It was the usual equatorial scorcher of a day, now amplified even more by bright reflections of sunlight off the ocean's surface.

I draped a large, red cotton bandanna over my head,

under my white baseball cap, in an effort to create a little more shade. Zigzagging across the bay, I skirted alongside one vessel after another. There were about twenty-five touring ships in the harbor. The ships had names like the *Darwin Explorer*, the *Daphne*, the *Beagle* (how unoriginal), *Stella Maris*, *Sulidae*, *Flamingo*, and the *Lobo del Mar*. The name that was my favorite belonged to a large, white sailboat called the *Resting Cloud*. My red kayak was dwarfed by even the smallest of these tour boats. The harbor was so crowded that all the boats had to double anchor, both fore and aft, to avoid swinging into each other.

Palm trees lined part of Puerto Ayora's waterfront behind me, and further into the distance, behind the town, green slopes rose very gradually toward the central highlands. Seven vegetative zones were represented, from the arid zone at sea level, to the forested uplands. From late morning on, the lush highlands were always flirting with some degree of cloud cover.

Academy Bay is a concavity at the extreme southeastern end of Santa Cruz Island providing an ideal protected anchorage. Not too many years ago there were very few boats using the harbor. But during the past few decades the bay has been discovered by the international boating set. Mooring fees are very high and there are stiff regulations to contend with. Nevertheless, the lure of the Galapagos is irresistible to many of the yachting crowd.

Academy Bay and the surrounding coastal waters have numerous shallow areas, with lava rocks jutting either through, or near to, the surface, depending on the tides. The ocean swells, when hitting these shallows, generate waves which then crash onto the shore.

Just before I reached the far side of the harbor as I paddled southwest, a group of seven golden rays swam by just below the surface on the left side of the kayak. They remained in formation, moving their "wings" in a slow rhythm that had the grace of ballet dancers.

As I left the protected harbor behind, I could see the surf breaking about one hundred yards off shore. I paddled out beyond that point into deeper and calmer water. Several flying fish leapt from the surface right in front of the kayak's bow , streaking sideways a few feet before falling back into the water.

I paddled my way along the coast, keeping to the

calm stretches where there were no waves.

Punta Estrada was barely over a mile from where I had rented the kayak, yet it seemed like it was on an entirely different island rather than just across the bay.

There were nearly vertical black lava cliffs, fronting the southern border of the bay. On the cliff tops grew the giant endemic prickly pear cactus, *Opuntia echios*, which can attain a height of thirty. Darwin mentioned this species of cactus several times in his journal, being impressed by its size. He never visited Santa Cruz, the island whose coast I was now exploring, but on September 21, 1835, when on San Cristobal ,the first island he stopped at, he wrote about the species for the first time. In his October 11th journal entry, while on Santiago Island, his fourth and final Galapagos landfall, he wrote, "In rocky parts there were great numbers of a peculiar cactus, whose large oval leaves connected together, formed branches rising from a cylindrical trunk."

As I paddled beneath the cliffs, waves crashed against them about two hundred yards to my left. A jutting point of rock kept me safely in the lee. There were many creatures also taking advantage of this calm zone. I maneuvered the kayak in close to the rock face, and on a small ledge, only two feet above my head, a young sea lion lounged in the sun. He sat up, gave me a surprised look, then collapsed back to sleep. His mother was tucked into a shady fold of the lava rock beneath him.

I was able to approach very closely to a group of six blue-footed boobies. Their dark, lance-like beaks, extending from thick, mottled, brownish-white heads and necks, made these amusing birds look longer than their actual measurement of two-and-a-half feet. They looked down at me from a distance of less than three feet. They stared, tilted their heads, looked at each other, then back at me again. Despite my extreme proximity, the boobies showed no inclination to fly off.

In his journal, Darwin wrote about "the extreme tameness of birds." In fact he devoted a full page to detailing this disposition, which he said was common to all the terrestrial species on the islands. Darwin took full advantage of this unwariness. He wrote, "All of them are often approached sufficiently near to be killed with a switch, and sometimes, as I myself tried, with a cap or a hat. A gun is here almost superfluous. It would appear that the birds of this Archipelago, not having as yet learnt that man is a more dangerous animal than the tortoise, disregard him."

Although a rock point sheltered me from bearing the full brunt of the breaking waves, I did catch the swells that they were generated. In front of me was the entrance to a small canyon leading back to a grove of red mangroves. This narrow inlet was only twenty feet across, with thirty foot walls on either side. It went back for about a quarter-mile.

The inside of the canyon was a totally different universe. With a marine iguana swimming right in front of the kayak, this could have been a miniature version of Conan Doyle's *Lost World*. The iguana scampered out of the water and part way up the nearly vertical rock face, finding a resting place in the sun about four feet up the wall.

Darwin was able to deduce some of the life cycle of the marine iguana by examining the stomach contents of several that he captured. He found their stomachs distended with seaweed , and since he hadn't observed seaweed growing in any quantity on the tidal rocks, he guessed that it must grow at the "bottom of the sea at some little distance from the coast." He went on to write, "If such be the case, the object of these animals occasionally going out to sea is explained." An anomaly in behavior that was more difficult for Darwin to explain was that "when frightened it will not enter the water."

When I neared the mangroves at the far end of the passage, a brown pelican plummeted headfirst into the water less than ten feet in front of me, startling me with the enormous splash as it crashed through the surface. It came up with lots of water and a small fish. A pelican can scoop up over 2.5 gallons of water in its pouch. The large bird then flew to the top of the lava wall and perched on the edge. The height provided a good vantage point from which it could observe prey in the water below.

The pelican was an adult, which was easy to determine by the white on its head. This continues as a long white stripe down both sides of its neck, reaching almost to its chest. Young pelicans are much more drab, being light brown above and paler below, and they entirely lack the white head and neck stripes.

After just a few moments of its bird's-eye

observation, the pelican dived again, coming even closer to the kayak. This time he came up empty-billed. Other pelicans sat along the cliff top, with giant cacti and blue sky behind them.

The sun was so vertical overhead that the narrow canyon's walls did not provide any shade at all at that time of day. In addition, the walls kept out any ocean breezes. It was like being in an oven. I was getting cooked, and occasionally felt fleeting moments of dizziness despite drinking plenty of water.

The short canyon contained various nooks and crannies. Dozens of colorful Sally lightfoot crabs backed off as I slowly glided alongside the lava walls. I noticed one pair mating underneath an overhanging ledge and was careful not to disturb them.

A lava heron hunched motionless on a rock that jutted just above the surface. This species is endemic to the Galapagos, being found along the rocky shores and mangrove swamps of the islands. It feeds on crabs, lizards, and small fish, quickly spearing them. This one was the epitome of intense concentration as he stared into the water. He was totally oblivious to my slow passage near him. His dark green plumage provided good camouflage against both the dark rock and the water. Only his yellow-orange legs made him noticeable. This 16-inch bird is the only endemic heron species in the Galapagos. Some scientists maintain that it is a subspecies of the striated heron.

Seven white-tipped reef sharks swam right underneath the kayak. During the day these sharks usually rest under rock ledges in reefs, hence their name. I wondered why they were cruising and not resting. This five-foot long shark has never been known to harm a human. It hangs out in the ocean shallows, often along beaches, and subsists on small fish, octopuses and crustaceans, hunting mostly at night. Darwin wrote that he collected "fifteen kinds of sea-fish". We do not know if the reef shark was one of them.

I paddled up and down the canyon a few more times. I found another lava heron, hunched and staring in catatonic fashion. This heron was younger than the first, with streaking through its brown feathers. I assumed that he was looking for small crabs and lizards among the rocks.

After I had been cooked in the sun for three-and-a-half hours I decided to leave the canyon and go explore elsewhere. A yellow warbler that alighted momentarily on a rock at the water's edge let out a brief, melodic song. A diminutive, stunningly attractive bird, the warbler has chestnut-brown coloration on its breast and on the top of its head. The rest of its body is bright yellow. Though small and delicate-looking, the yellow warbler is a tenacious carnivore which hunts down insects both on the ground and in the air.

As I sat perfectly still, watching the warbler, another small bird landed on the brim of my baseball cap. Darwin wrote in his journal, "Formerly the birds appear to have been even tamer that at present. A Mr. Cowly, in 1684, said that the 'Turtledoves were so tame, that they would often alight on our hats and arms, so as that we could take them alive, they not fearing man. A man in a morning's walk might kill six or seven dozen of these doves'." Of twenty-nine resident species of land birds in the archipelago, Darwin killed and collected twenty-six. The bird on my cap flew off to a mangrove branch. I took out my binoculars to identify it, and it turned out to be one of the thirteen species of endemic *Darwin's finches.* Nine of these species live on Santa

Cruz, but I could not tell one from the other.

Darwin did not realize that of the 26 land bird species he collected, 12 were different species of finches. He had assumed that all the birds he brought back were not closely related and, in fact, were not finches at all. About three months after the voyage ended, Darwin presented his specimen collection to the famous English ornithologist John Gould. Gould determined that the birds were a series of twelve ground finches and not, as Darwin had assumed, blackbirds and mockingbirds. Darwin had not even bothered to label the birds according to which island they had come from and had to cross reference with specimens collected by Captain Fitzroy and other members of the crew. Luckily they had kept better records than Darwin. Today, the thirteen Galapagos finches are all considered to be members of the family *Emberizidae* representing four distinct genera. Darwin did not actually conceive of his theory of natural selection until 1838, three years after he had returned from his voyage and after he had ample time to reflect on the implications of his bird collection.

As I resumed paddling toward the canyon entrance,

a group of five golden rays glided past, just below the surface. And I could make out three more reef sharks near the bottom. I passed within two feet of one of the lava herons. He continued staring at the water, lost in his hunt.

With a few more paddle strokes I left the canyon and returned to the outside world of ocean swells. Hugging the coast to the left, I came upon a half-mile wide lagoon with a small rock islet out in the middle. Most of the lagoon was surrounded by mangroves, except for the rocky north end which had waves breaking from various directions.

As my red kayak cut through the water toward the rock islet, I could see that there were about two dozen blue-footed boobies gathered in a small area. One of the birds quickly caught my attention. It had a clear plastic bag around its neck with its head sticking up through a tear in the plastic. Somehow this booby was able to fly normally. It managed to get airborne without a problem, bag in tow. Hopefully the plastic would tear free before it became repositioned in some more lethal fashion. For the moment, that particular bird was an unwitting ambassador for the wildlife community, graphically conveying a message of conservation in a way more effective than words to all who might catch a glimpse of it.

Blue-footed booby with plastic bag stuck on its neck

It was now 4 PM. The sun was still plenty high in the sky and the air temperature remained hot. I realized that I had been sitting in the kayak continuously for six hours. I exited the lagoon by paddling close to a small island. Waves broke all around the island's ocean-facing side, but I could tuck in the lee, staying clear of any surf.

Additional tour boats pulled into the harbor as I again zigzagged through the smorgasbord of vessels. To the jumble of anchored boats was added the noisy confusion of the constant comings and goings of dinghies. The harbor was a beehive of activity and in the midst of this frenetic bustle, one could hear the blare of loud Spanish music coming from the deck of one of the larger ships.

As I approached the *Red Mangrove Inn*, the tide was at its highest and part of the little dock that I had launched from was now submerged. The shallow channel I had paddled out through, seven or so hours earlier, no longer existed. Water completely covered all the rocks.

Chapter Eight
A PEN OF TORTUGAS

As ironic as it may sound, there are not really many places in the Galapagos Islands where a visitor can readily view wild Galapagos tortoises. The population of the animal for which the islands are best known is today only a fraction of what it was in past centuries. For this sad state of affairs we can thank the pirates, whalers, and sealers of yesteryear. They killed tortoises by the thousands to provide food for their ships. The crew of the *Beagle* captured forty-eight tortoises and loaded them aboard the ship, thereby providing themselves with nearly five tons of meat.

Today there are about 15,000 to 18,000 giant tortoises remaining in the Galapagos. They are distributed over six different islands encompassing some very inhospitable terrain. The situation does not lend itself to very easy tortoise observation.

There are, in fact, only two good sites in the entire archipelago at which you can reliably see tortoises in the wild. One of these locations, the El Chato Tortoise Reserve on Santa Cruz Island, requires a hot, two-hour hike before you arrive at a good viewing area, and even then there are no guarantees that you will encounter more than an occasional tortoise. The other site is much more difficult to reach. It requires a trip to Puerto Villamil on remote Isabela Island, and once there hiring a guide and boat. You must then embark on a seven-hour coastal sea journey, followed by an all-day trudge up the slopes of Alcedo Volcano and an overnight campout in the rainy highlands. Thousands of tortoises still inhabit the Alcedo region.

I visited the *El Chato* Reserve four times, encountering a marginal number of tortoises, all of which were afraid of me. Upon my approach they quickly withdrew into their shells, giving off a loud and disturbing hissing sound as they did so. Darwin noticed the same thing during his first encounter with a wild tortoise, which took place on San Cristobal Island on September 21, 1835. He wrote in his diary that day, "One was eating a Cactus & then quietly walked away. The other gave a deep & loud hiss & then drew back his head."

Alcedo has traditionally been a great tortoise viewing area. Unfortunately, the volcano had become overrun with feral goats — about 100,000 of them by 1998 (there were none in 1983). The goats had caused a devastating amount of defoliation, prompting the Park Service to close the area to visitation while rangers attempted to eradicate the goats by shooting them as part of Project Isabela. This energetic initiative was successfully completed by 2006, with all the goats being eliminated. Even during the 18th century, feral goats were already spreading in numbers on Floreana Island. Darwin made mention of them (and pigs) in his journal entry of September 24, 1835.

The only other guaranteed access to tortoises, besides El Chato and Alcedo, were to the captive groups located 1.5 miles from downtown Puerto Ayora, and at the smaller rearing facility located at Puerto Villamil on Isabela island.

The Charles Darwin Research Station (CDRS) was established just outside of Puerto Ayora on the island of Santa Cruz in 1960, one year after Ecuador created Galapagos National Park. Initially, the purpose of the center was scientific research, but the station's mission was quickly expanded to include saving the tortoise (and later land iguanas) from extinction. A tortoise rearing facility was constructed.

There was no question that the tortoises desperately needed saving. Of the original fourteen different races of the giant Galapagos tortoise, three have gone extinct.

In 1965 the CDRS began a captive breeding program for the Galapagos tortoise. The program became a joint venture with the Ecuadorian National

Park Service three years later.

Thus pure research biologists found themselves in the business of raising tortoises — as many as possible in as short a time frame as possible. In the wild, sometimes no hatchlings at all are able to survive due to predation by feral rats and dogs. So scientists go out and collect all the tortoise eggs that they can find and bring them back to the research station. The eggs are then incubated artificially and the vulnerable hatchlings are protected in captivity until they are four years old. At that age their shells are hard enough and large enough so that neither rats nor dogs can kill them, and they are then returned to the wild, to their island of origin.

The Espanola Island success story is particularly heartening. In the early 1970's there were only fourteen members of the Espanola race of tortoises remaining alive. The entire subspecies seemed headed for certain extinction. Scientists captured all fourteen individuals, added one additional Espanola tortoise donated by the San Diego Zoo, and began breeding them at the CDRS. As of 1990, 320 Espanola tortoises had been re-released back onto their home island. This is one of the few times in the history of the world that a species once eradicated in the wild has been successfully reintroduced back into its historic wild habitat.

In the course of breeding the captive tortoises, researchers made a remarkable discovery: the temperature at which the eggs are incubated is of paramount importance in determining the sex of the offspring. In one of nature's more bizarre flirtations with the phenomenon of sex, it turns out that cooler eggs become male tortoises and warmer eggs female. All eggs that are incubated at 38 degrees Centigrade (100.4 degrees Fahrenheit) will hatch out as males. By adding just a few increments of heat and incubating the eggs at 39.5 degrees Centigrade (103.1 degrees Fahrenheit), every egg that hatches will produce a female tortoise. Strange but true.

The researchers were quick to take advantage of this quirk of reproductive biology. They regulate incubation temperatures so that of all tortoises hatched out, two-thirds will be female and one-third male. Population dynamics dictates that such a blend of the sexes will maximize the number of tortoises in the wild.

Through this strict manipulation, 1400 captivity-reared tortoises had been raised and released back into the wild by 1992, and 2800 by 2000. This program achieves a remarkable eighty percent survival rate.

As a fringe benefit, the CDRS has pens full of tortoises that tourists may observe. At any one time there are dozens of young tortoises waiting to be released into the wild. On most days, throngs of visitors from some of the ninety or so tour boats are shuttled ashore to walk through the expansive and picturesque grounds of the CDRS, and to view the famed creatures for which the islands are named.

There are two separate large pens that are the main crowd pleasers. Both of the pens are very natural-looking enclosures with plenty of lava rock, an uneven landscape, and giant *opuntia* cacti. Each pen is perhaps a half acre in size, and each has a small pond.

In one of these pens resides "Lonesome George", arguably the world's most famous tortoise. He used to live on Pinta Island, one of the northernmost of the archipelago. Pinta is the last island that Darwin laid eyes on before finally departing from the Galapagos. In his journal entry for October 19, 1835, he wrote: "...steered for two small Islands which lie 100 miles to the North of the rest of the group." He was referring to Marchena and Pinta. He never got to set foot on Pinta. After sailing close to that island, the *Beagle* set sail for Tahiti.

Some of the elimination of Lonesome George's relatives was accomplished by human predation. But even more insidious a factor was the introduction on to Pinta Island of feral goats by local fishermen in the late 1950's. The statistics are not only distressing, but so extraordinary as to defy belief: just *three* introduced goats — a male and two females — multiplied to the astronomical number of *thirty-eight thousand* in only fourteen years. Goats are able to achieve this incredible feat by reaching sexual maturity rapidly and by then having two litters per year, with 2-3 kids per litter. The deluge of goats then, quite literally, eats the tortoises out of house and home.

Goats have already been successfully removed from eight of the Galapagos Islands. They were thought to have been eradicated from Pinta Island in 1990, but in August 1995, a small group of feral goats was discovered on the island again. When they found this out, Park Service personnel set to work right away trying to eliminate them.

At seventy years of age, having only lived half his life, Lonesome George was captured by researchers in 1972 and brought to the CDRS. Since all Pinta females have forever disappeared from the face of the earth, scientists imported two female tortoises from Volcan Wolf. These females belonged to the farthest northern subspecies on Isabela Island, to a race of Galapagos tortoises that researchers felt was closest, of the remaining races, to George's own. The two Isabelans were put into George's enclosure. In 2008, after 36 years of celibacy, mating finally took place. However the clutch of five eggs proved to be infertile. So in January of 2011 two new females, thought to be even more closely related to George's Geochelone abigonde line, were brought in to replace the original two. Researchers now have their fingers crossed.

The other enclosure, even larger than George's, contained five adult male tortoises, each over fifty years old and weighing at least 550 pounds. These five males had previously been kept as pets, but were surrendered voluntarily to authorities upon the establishment of Galapagos National Park. The origins of these tortoises was not certain. So rather than risk polluting the gene pool, it was decided to keep them out of the breeding program entirely. They are now simply tourist attractions. The public is permitted to wander around inside the enclosure. Exposure to thousands of visitors over the years has habituated the tortoises to humans to the extent that, unlike their wild brethren, they don't retract their heads or hiss when in close proximity to people.

After a few tough hikes through the *El Chato* Tortoise Reserve, the limitation of photo ops with wild tortoises had become obvious. One couldn't approach non-habituated tortoises closely without having them retract their heads immediately, a movement always accompanied by that demonic sounding hiss resulting from the expulsion of air from their lungs. As unlikely as it may sound, tortoises have no respiratory muscles. Air moves into and out of their lungs only in a passive response to body movements, similar to how an accordion works.

After having my fill of frustrating photo sessions in *El Chato* with one retracted head after another, I gravitated toward the research station for tortoise photography.

During the heat of the day, which means from about eight or nine o'clock onward, giant tortoises — in captivity as well as in the wild — seek shade and become the sluggish creatures most of us assume them to be all of the time. But first thing in the morning they are quite active, interacting with each other to an amazing degree.

During the early hours of the day they are very alert and appear to notice every sound, despite Charles Darwin's claim, in a letter dated September 29, 1835, that they are "absolutely deaf." They stretch their necks out to an incredible 2.5 ft or so in length, and stand high on their elephant-like feet to survey their surroundings. They fight with each other, eat voraciously and, in the absence of females, the males attempt to copulate with each other, accompanied by loud, roaring grunts. These enormous reptiles are not slouches.

On several mornings I visited the research station at dawn. The dirt path leading past the INEFAN (Institute of Ecuadorian Forestry And Nature) sign crosses a stretch of lowland desert that at that early hour is noisy with the songs of many birds. The yellow warbler, mockingbird, Galapagos flycatcher, and a variety of Darwin's finches all flit about. I saw a cactus finch land, appropriately enough, on one of the spiny pads of a giant prickly pear cactus.

Cactus finch (one of "Darwin's Finches")

Along with the candelabra cactus, the giant prickly pear is a prominent part of the landscape of the archipelago. It has a bare base like a tree which rises about six feet before any branching occurs. The cactus arms, from which grow the flat, well-needled pads, sag back somewhat toward the earth, but still usually remain at least a few feet above the ground. The pads break off fairly easily at their point of attachment, but are so thoroughly covered with nasty spines that handling a pad is a tricky affair. After trial and error, I finally discovered that I could carry one pad at a time by holding it between just my thumb and index finger and gripping the pad's base.

I went about collecting cactus pads until I had a respectable stack. Inside the enclosure the large tortoises were resting in the pond. One raised his head and looked at me.

I carried a single spiny pad and placed it on a nearby lava rock. A tortoise quickly walked right over to it, chomping down and practically inhaling the pad, spines and all, in his enthusiasm to eat. I found it surprising how juicy a dry-looking cactus can be. As he devoured the meal, the pad oozed copious amounts of liquid. It seemed to hold as much water as a soggy sponge. Darwin had observed that where water was scarce the giant tortoise could survive by eating cactus pads. By watching the a tortoise feed, it was easy to see how this could be true.

I retrieved another pad and this caught the attention of the other tortoises in the enclosure. They all headed in my direction.

The tortoises were eager to eat the cactus pads

Three of the tortoises stretched out their necks, like king cobras being charmed. There was a standoff, with the tortoises all looking at each other menacingly.

I clicked off a few photos and then quickly retrieved the remainder of the cactus pads and handed them out to the various tortoises until they were all devoured.

I walked along the path leading back into Puerto Ayora, passing a souvenir stand and the small CDRS museum. I encountered the morning's first tour group and overheard their naturalist guide lecturing that the common ancestor of the giant tortoise originated on San Cristobal Island. The group continued on past me.

Before reaching town, I took a side path down to

the bay. Two brown pelicans sat along the lava rock shoreline while lava lizards scampered about them. Sally lightfoot crabs crawled erratically over the black rocks, and perhaps a dozen young marine iguanas faced the sun and absorbed its warmth. A larger iguana swam just offshore in the mild surf. A few blue-footed boobies took turns plunge-diving for breakfast, about a football field's length offshore. The scene before me was much the same, I imagined, as when these islands were first discovered in 1535 by Fray Tomas de Berlanga, the Bishop of Panama, a full 300 years before Darwin's visit.

Chapter Nine
THIRTY-SIX DAYS

Charles Darwin visited the Galapagos Islands from September 15 to October 20, 1835. It is incredible that a person could develop a theory that would shake the foundations of science and so profoundly affect the world based upon a mere five weeks of observation. During that time he visited only four islands while collecting his innumerable biological specimens. Some of the crew, including the ship's captain, Robert Fitzroy, also gathered their own specimens. (The most crucial collection was of the thirteen different species of finches. Feeding, and thus beak variations, proved to be the key that Darwin needed).

Darwin did not immediately realize just how

significant those collections would become. Nor did he realize the ramifications on scientific thought that his astonishingly brief visit would have. At the time he was simply a young — albeit curious, competent, and thorough — 26 year old naturalist adventuring around the world. He was 22 at the start of the voyage, in December 1831.

It was not until 1859, a quarter-century after his Galapagos visit, that Darwin finally completed a synthesis of his past observations and released *On The Origin of Species.*

When I had landed at the Baltra Airport on January 31, 1996, I mused over the notion that I might end up spending as much time in the Galapagos Islands as Darwin.

Darwin was fortunate to have been invited on the voyage. He came close to not going even after receiving the invitation. At first he turned it down when his father, wanting him to become a clergyman, objected strongly to his participation. But the next day, one of Darwin's uncles intervened on his behalf and convinced Darwin's father to allow him to go. Darwin recounts the episode in his autobiography and wrote that his father told him, when finally approving the trip, "They tell me you are very clever."

During my final days on Santa Cruz Island I continued to observe and photograph the wildlife. Marine iguanas start appearing on the rocks early in the morning, trying to absorb all the solar warmth they can get.

Small lava lizards scurry about. Lava herons land and begin searching for fish. Pelicans sun themselves as dozens of Sally lightfoot crabs crawl about. Swallowtail gulls arrive in pairs. Overhead, magnificent frigatebirds soar, waiting to rob other birds of their meals, or to snatch fish scraps discarded by nearby Pelican Cove fishermen. These consummate flyers have the largest wingspan-to-weight ratio of any bird in the world. Blue-footed boobies plunge-dive into the ocean like torpedoes, disappearing beneath the surface, then bobbing up like corks about ten seconds later, usually with small fish in their mouths. The wildlife spectacle is never-ending.

Lava Lizard

One species that was not so readily observed was the land iguana. While the marine iguana is ubiquitous, the land iguana is much more difficult to locate. Unlike the marine iguana, which lives on most of the islands in the archipelago, the land iguana, *Conolophus subcristatus*, is native to only six of the islands. A second species of land iguana, *Conolophus pallidus*, is found only on Santa Fe Island.

Darwin had his first encounter with land iguanas on

Isabela (Albemarle) Island on October 1, 1835. "We here have another large Reptile in great numbers," he wrote. They are hideous animals; but are considered good food: this day forty were collected." Darwin recognized that this species was confined to only a few islands, and noted that observation in his journal.

Santa Cruz is one of the six islands that this iguana lives on, but they are not commonly found in the wild around the town site of Puerto Ayora. Although once common, the land iguana population in many areas has been greatly reduced or entirely wiped out by feral dogs. Such was the case on Santa Cruz. In 1976 wild dogs killed 500 land iguanas at Conway Bay and then additional iguanas at Cartago Bay. The Charles Darwin Research Station and the Galapagos National Park Service rescued the remaining iguanas and with them they began a captive breeding program in Puerto Ayora. The wild dogs were eliminated and some of the land iguanas have been reintroduced into the wild since 1988.

In Darwin's time, before the introduction of so many feral animals, land iguanas were just as numerous as their marine cousins. When Darwin was on Santiago

Island, he wrote in his journal on October 9, 1835 that "There are infinite numbers of the large yellow herbivorous Lizard. The burrows of this animal are so very numerous that we had difficulty in finding a spot to pitch the tents."

I had seen my only land iguana on the final day of the *Angelique* cruise when we stopped for a brief visit at South Plaza Island, just off the northeast coastline of Santa Cruz. The small island is all lowlands and very dry. Land iguanas inhabit only the driest parts of the islands where they live. By eating predominantly the juicy pads and fruit of the prickly pear cactus they can survive without any supplemental water for over a year if necessary. As Darwin had observed, they utilize burrows as nesting sites and also to retire into at night to conserve body heat.

In observing the land iguanas, Darwin wrote that "...I caught many by the tail, and they never tried to bite me. If two are placed on the ground and held together, they will fight, and bite each other till blood is drawn."

Before leaving South Plaza we walked up to the edge of a low cliff and were able to observe swallow-tail gulls, an Audubon shearwater, and a red-billed tropicbird with its long, thin tail feathers.

My visit to South Plaza was already a few weeks in the past and my stay in the Galapagos was slowly coming to an end.

Darwin may have sailed for five years, but when it came to roughing it, he was no Ernest Shackleton. Sailing is a "tedious waste" he wrote, adding that someone had better have a good reason before undertaking such an uncomfortable journey. He was often seasick. The *Beagle* first sailed on December 27, 1831 and he became seasick the very next day, writing that , "The misery is excessive."

Unlike many stoic explorers, Darwin complained of "want of room, seclusion, rest, small luxuries, domesticity, and music." When near Valparaiso, Chile, a point in time that was more than a year before the naturalist was to reach the Galapagos, and more than two years before his journey would conclude with a return home to England, he complained in a letter to his sister, "The first and best news I have to tell is that our voyage has at last a definite and certain end fixed to it. I was beginning to grow quite miserable." Soon after he had written the letter, the *Beagle* docked in Valparaiso and Darwin managed to get off the ship and spend twelve weeks on land.

Darwin was often unhappy. He would take a break from expeditioning whenever the opportunity presented itself. He enthusiastically welcomed the opportunity for time-outs. Previously, he had been quoted as saying, "I should have thought myself mad to give up the first days of partridge shooting for geology or any other science."

In addition to the 1834 Valparaiso hiatus, from April through July of 1835 — two months before visiting the Galapagos — Darwin managed to take a four-month leave from the ship, during which time he tramped around between Coquimbo and Copiupo in Chile. It's not clear as to whether or not Darwin was looking forward to the trip when it finally came time to leave mainland South America and head for the Galapagos. On September 7, 1835, Captain Fitzroy raised anchor and took a week to sail the *Beagle* from Callao, just outside Lima, Peru, to Chatham Island (San Cristobal). For all we know, Darwin may have objected to the journey.

The man may have been every inch a genius, but he

loved certain pedestrian pursuits and was not embarrassed to say so. When he studied at Cambridge University, no one could accuse him of being the proverbial bookworm. "My time was sadly wasted there," he wrote, "and worse than wasted." He had a passion for shooting, hunting, and riding horses. In one of his letters from that period he commented, "I do not believe that anyone could have shown more zeal for the most holy cause than I did for shooting birds."

By the time Darwin landed on Chatham Island on September 15, 1835, he apparently was in need of some diversion and amusement and took to riding on the backs of the giant tortoises. It is difficult to picture this celebrated scientist partaking of such a stunt, but that he did so is well documented. He makes no effort to cover up his shenanigans, and is remarkably candid in his journal entry of September 29, 1835: "I frequently got on their backs, and then, giving a few raps on the hinder part of their shells, they would rise up and walk away."

During my Galapagos visit I mailed about 25 postcards home to my wife (although, I found out later, only one managed to get through). Darwin's diary, later published as *The Voyage Of The Beagle* in 1839, was originally written with home correspondence in mind. In his autobiography years later, he recalled: "During some part of the day I wrote in my Journal, and took such pains in describing carefully and vividly all that I had seen. My Journal served also, in part, as letters to my home, and portions were sent to England whenever there was an opportunity."

The reality of ocean travel in the early nineteenth century was that it wasn't very conducive to remaining healthy. For much of his travels aboard the 90-foot Beagle, Darwin had to live in cramped quarters with seventy-five other crewmen. He also had to spend a considerable amount of time with his charitable but schizoid captain, Robert Fitzroy. Darwin described Fitzroy as having an "unfortunate temper." He further commented that, "Fitzroy was a man who has the most consummate skill in looking at everything and everybody in a perverted manner." Can you imagine five years of sailing with a man like that in charge?

A narrow path with lava rocks stacked on both sides leads from Puerto Ayora for about two miles until it reaches the beach at *Tortuga Bay*. One can then hike west along the shoreline for another mile or so. The white sand beach is magnificent. To the north are the gentle, green cloud-covered slopes of the interior highlands. To the south and east can be seen the islands of Floreana and Santa Fe. Floreana was the second island that Darwin visited, from September 23-27, 1835.

In the heat of the day, especially during late morning, the *Tortuga Bay* beach is visited by many marine iguanas which seem to make a daily passage over the sand, from east to west (I assume they make the reverse trek some time during the late evening). Sanderlings--small, white sandpiper-type birds--work the water's edge, running back and forth while probing for small marine worms, crustaceans and mollusks. Ghost crabs scurry about by the dozens. They are surprisingly alert and quick.

Marine Iguana on the beach at Tortuga Bay

Ghost Crab

Brown pelicans glide smoothly just inches above the waves, as close as they can possibly get to the water without actually touching it. When they soar higher up and spot a fish just beneath the surface, they plunge-dive, with all the grace of a crashing airplane.

In the early evening, about five hundred whimbrels gather at the west end of the beach, amassing in one large grouping. The whimbrel is a big shorebird, eighteen inches long and possessing a four inch downward-curved bill. The bird is a mottled grayish-brown, with a horizontally striped head and a dark eye line. Whimbrels nest on open tundra in Alaska and fly south to spend the winter months on warm coastal beaches.

Whimbrel

Hundreds of cattle egrets fly down from their day's foraging in the highlands to roost in a concentrated cluster of red mangroves--the very same mangroves every day--in a cove off of the bay. The all-white egrets thickly cover the mangroves among whose branches they roost. This stocky species of egret is native to Africa, and did not appear in the Galapagos until 1965. The species is now distributed worldwide. It had first made its way to South America about the same time that Darwin visited.

Interestingly, at 5:45 PM, not a single cattle egret will

have arrived to roost. Yet just thirty minutes later, it's a full house, with the mangroves' branches filled with a riot of birds. The timing is incredibly precise, day after day.

One evening, a dead bull sea lion washed up on the beach. Near the sea lion were sea turtle tracks that led from the ocean, over the sand, to low dunes just above the high tide line, indicating where a turtle had excavated a pit and laid and buried her eggs.

I spent several evenings visiting the beach and just appreciating the wildlife, often not even bothering to take photographs.

Darwin was an enthusiastic collector and observer and a formidable scientific thinker. Yet his chronically poor health prevented him from finishing projects as quickly as he might have otherwise. His five-year voyage ended on Oct 2, 1836. By March 1837 he had made the determination that living separately actually changed species, and by the following year, he conceived of the theory of natural selection. Yet it took him nine years to write *The Voyage of the Beagle* (1845), twenty-four years to write *The Origin of Species* (1859), and ten years to jot down his autobiographical notes, which were finally published five years posthumously, in 1887.

Darwin was well aware of his talents. In his autobiography he wrote, "My habits are methodical, and this has been of not a little use for my particular line of work. My success as a man of science has been determined by complex and diversified mental qualities and conditions. Of these, the most important have been the love of science, unbounded patience in long reflecting over any subject, industry in observing and collecting facts, and a fair share of invention as well as of common sense."

Darwin's intellect was awesome, but he was not the person you would want to call upon to complete a task quickly. *The Origin of Species* might have never been completed at all if it wasn't for some serious prodding from his academic confidant, the geologist Sir Charles Lyell. Darwin had written only a short sketch of *Origins* by 1844, and then between 1856 and 1858 got it perhaps half done.

Then in 1858 a naturalist colleague, Alfred Russel Wallace, out of the blue, sent him a letter from Malaysia saying that he, Wallace, had discovered a fascinating theory about evolution and natural selection. I'm sure that upon reading the letter, Darwin's eyes must have gone wide and his lower jaw must have dropped.

Darwin in 1854, at age 45, five years before On The Origin of Species was published

Darwin, to his credit, was a faithful and honest friend. He did not attempt to steal Wallace's thunder. He politely deferred to Wallace, and sent a copy of the letter to Professor Lyell. Lyell then rounded up the famous botanist, Joseph Hooker, and the two professors decided that Wallace and Darwin should present a joint paper to London academia's *Linnaean Society*, on the topic of natural selection.

In the meantime, Darwin went into high gear. After procrastinating for twenty-two years, he sat down and cranked out *Origins* in just thirteen months (at age 51). It's amazing what a little competition and friendly rivalry can accomplish. Darwin had readily admitted in his autobiography that "...I was ambitious to take a fair place among scientific men."

My own expectations were a lot more modest. I settled for capturing the best photographic images that I could obtain and for spending an inspired time in an exotic location inhabited by fearless creatures.

Darwin spent an often difficult five years in order to eventually arrive at his moment of greatness. Years later, when writing his autobiography, he wrote fondly of his boat journey and what it had meant to his development as a scientist. He made no mention that sharing a small boat cabin for a long period of time is claustrophobic at best. Or that his psyche had not been helped by the fact that his cabin-mates were two teenagers, or that he had to put up with a moody and volatile ship's captain, someone with whom he was constantly at philosophical and emotional odds. Captain Fitzroy saw Darwin as incorrigible. He was a rogue intellectual and spiritual thorn in the Captain's side, both during and after the voyage of the *Beagle*.

Fitzroy, three years older than Darwin, was an intensely religious man. He believed rigidly and absolutely in every word contained in the Bible. His interpretation of Scriptures was literal. The world and all its creatures had been created in six days. Period. Fitzroy knew that Darwin had been studying theology at Cambridge and that Robert Darwin, his father, intended for his son to join the clergy. When Fitzroy invited Darwin on the expedition, he had no idea that the budding scientist preferred hunting and bug collecting to religious studies, or to any studies, for that matter.

Thus Captain Robert Fitzroy made one of the most outrageous philosophical blunders of all time. He invited Darwin along because he assumed that the religious-appearing naturalist would substantiate the Bible and confirm Genesis. The emotional ramifications of Fitzroy's stupendous miscalculation was to haunt him for the rest of his life, ending in his death by suicide on April 30, 1865 at the age of 59.

For being on a sea voyage, Charles Darwin actually spent an extraordinary amount of time on land. During the course of the sixty months of the expedition, a full eighteen months were spent on solid ground. Darwin's dissatisfaction with a steady diet of boat life was further aggravated by his father's relentless badgering, through mail correspondence, urging his son to quit the expedition and come home.

To his credit, despite the lack of amenities, Darwin persisted. He took leave when he felt he needed it — and could get it — but he always returned to the ship. That persistence allowed him those 35 historically special days in the Galapagos, days sandwiched as almost an afterthought between Callao, Peru, and Tahiti.

Darwin, in looking back on that period in his life, wrote what is today obvious to everyone: "The voyage of the *Beagle* has been by far the most important event in my life, and has determined my whole career. I have always felt that I owe to the voyage the first real training or education of my mind; I was led to attend closely to several branches of natural history, and thus my powers of observation were improved. I worked to the utmost during the voyage from the mere pleasure of investigation."

When Darwin left the Galapagos Islands on October 20, 1835, Captain Fitzroy sailed the *Beagle* southwestward for 3200 miles before making landfall in Tahiti three and a half weeks and a number of consumed tortoises later.

My thirty-fifth day in the Galapagos was March 6, 1996. I outstayed Darwin the next day and got on a flight going home.

###

BIBLIOGRAPHY

Bowlby, John. Charles Darwin: A New Life. New York & London: W.W. Norton & Company. 1990.

Brown, Frank Burch. The Evolution of Darwin's Religious Views. Macon, Georgia. MercerUniversity Press. 1986

Darwin, Charles. The Voyage of the Beagle. London. John Murray. 1845.

Desmond, Adrian and Moore, James. Darwin. Great Britain. Michael Joseph Ltd. 1991

Moorehead, Alan. Darwin and the Beagle. New York and Evanston. Harper & Row. 1969

Jackson, Michael H. Galapagos: A Natural History. Calgary, Alberta, Canada: University of Calgary Press. 1993.

Jastrow, Robert and Karey, Kenneth. The Essential Darwin. Boston and Toronto. LittleBrown and Company. 1984

Rachowiecki, Rob. Ecuador & The Galapagos Islands. Hawthorn, Victoria, Australia: Lonely Planet Publications, 1992.

Ralling, Christopher. The Voyage of Charles Darwin. New York: Mayflower Books. 1979.

Ridley, Mark. The Darwin Reader. New York and London. W.W. Norton & Co. 1987

Stewart, Paul D. Galapagos: The Islands That Changed The World. New Haven & London. Yale University Press. 2006.

Tierney, Jr., Lawrence, McPhee, Stephen and Papadakis Maxine. Current Medical Diagnosis and Treatment. Stamford, CT. Appleton & Lange. 1996

NAMES OF THE GALAPAGOS ISLANDS

(Old English names are in parentheses)

Baltra (South Seymour)

Bartolome (Bartholomew)

Daphne Major (single name only)

Darwin (Culpepper)

Espanola (Hood)

Genovesa (Tower)

Fernandina (Narborough)

Floreana (Charles)

Isabela (Albemarle)

Marchena (Bindloe)

North Seymour (single name only)

Pinzon (Duncan)

Pinta (Abingdon)

Rabida (Jervis)

San Cristobal (Chatham)

Santa Cruz (Indefatigable)

Santa Fe (Barrington)

Santiago (James)

South Plaza (single name only)

Wolf (Wenman)

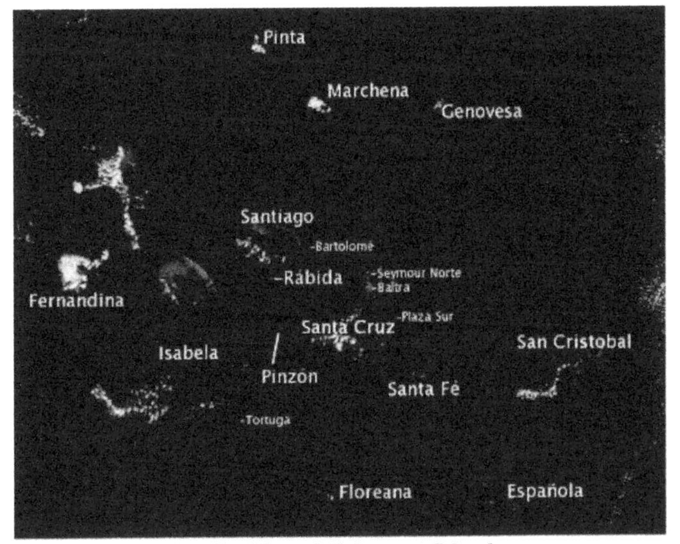

Satellite Map of Galapagos Islands

PHOTO CREDITS

ALL PHOTOS ARE BY THE AUTHOR EXCEPT FOR THE FOLLOWING:

p.6: Wikimedia Commons, Public Domain

p.20: Watercolor by George Richmond, 1838, Wikimedia Commons, public domain

p.25: Drawing by unknown artist, done circa 1889-90. Wikimedia Commons, public domain

p.29: Wendy Newman created this map from a description of the route taken by the *Angelique*

p.42: Painting by Johannes Gerardus Keulemans (1842-1912), Wikimedia Commons, public domain

p.57: A. Flores Lopez, Wikimedia Commons, public domain

p.137: Wikimedia Commons, public domain

p.144: Wikimedia Commons, public domain

p.152: Wikimedia Commons, public domain

p.153: Wikimedia Commons, public domain

p.156: Wikimedia Commons, public domain

p.167: Wikimedia Commons, public domain

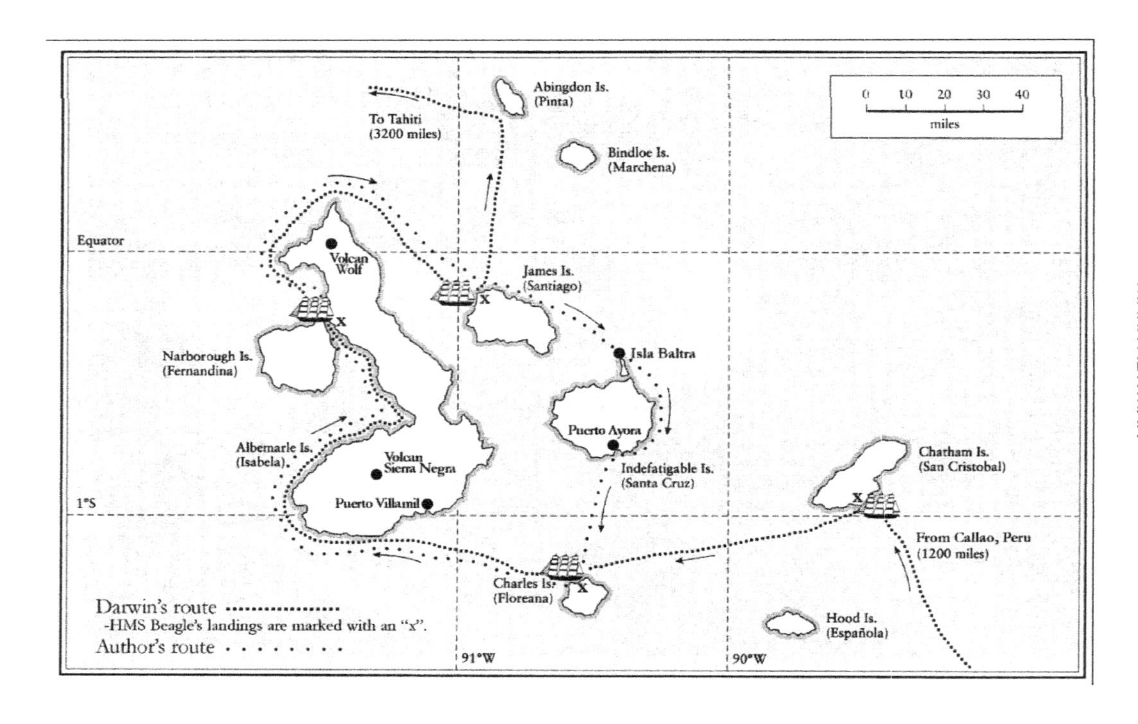
0 10 20 30 40
miles
To Tahiti
(3200 miles)
Abingdon Is.
(Pinta)
Bindloe Is.
(Marchena)
Equator
Volcan
Wolf
James Is.
(Santiago)
Isla Baltra
Narborough Is.
(Fernandina)
Puerto Ayora
Albemarle Is.
(Isabela)
Volcan
Sierra Negra
Indefatigable Is.
(Santa Cruz)
Chatham Is.
(San Cristobal)
1°S
Puerto Villamil
From Callao, Peru
(1200 miles)
Charles Is.
(Floreana)
Darwin's route
-HMS Beagle's landings are marked with an "x".
Author's route
Hood Is.
(Española)
91°W
90°W

Made in the USA
Middletown, DE
27 October 2022